Islamic Rulings Regarding the Qur'ān

Fatāwa from
The Permanent Committee of Scholars, Saudi Arabia

Translated by
Faisal Ibn Muhammad

ISBN 1 898649 57 X

British Library Cataloguing in Publication Data.
A catalogue record for this book is available from the British Library.

Published: Al-Hidaayah Publishing and Distribution

Distributed by: Al-Hidaayah Publishing and Distribution
P.O. Box 3332
Birmingham
United Kingdom
B10 0UH

Tel: 0121 753 1889
Fax: 0121 753 2422
Website: www.al-hidaayah.co.uk
Email: mail@al-hidaayah.co.uk

Contents

Transliteration Table

Consonants,

ء	’	د	d	ض	ḍ	ك	k
ب	b	ذ	dh	ط	ṭ	ل	l
ت	t	ر	r	ظ	ẓ	م	m
ث	th	ز	z	ع	‘	ن	n
ج	j	س	s	غ	gh	ه	h
ح	ḥ	ش	sh	ف	f	و	w
خ	kh	ص	ṣ	ق	q	ي	y

Vowels, diphthongs, etc.

Short:	ـَ	a	ـِ	i	ـُ	u
Long:	ـَا	ā	ـِي	ī	ـُو	ū
diphthongs:			ـَىْ	ay	ـَوْ	aw

Islamic Rulings Regarding the Qur'ān

Rulings Regarding those Who Abandon the Qur'ān

Reading the Qur'ān: Is it Compulsory?

1-Q: Is reciting the Qur'ān wājib (compulsory) upon us or just mustaḥabb (recommended)? Once, when this question was put forward, I heard someone say that it is wājib; but if it is indeed wājib, then many people are sinning because they have abandoned the Qur'ān – i.e., they never recite it. What then is the Islamic ruling concerning abandoning the Qur'ān and what is the ruling concerning reciting it?

A: All praise is for Allāh alone, and may His prayers and salutations be upon Muḥammad, his family, and his companions.

What is legislated for the Muslim is for him to consistently and frequently recite the Qur'ān, to a degree that he is capable of, thus applying the verse:

ٱتْلُ مَآ أُوحِىَ إِلَيْكَ مِنَ ٱلْكِتَٰبِ

> Recite (O Muḥammad (ﷺ)) what has been revealed to you of the Book (the Qur'ān).[1]

In the following verse, Allāh (ﷻ) relates what His Prophet Muḥammad (ﷺ) said:

وَأُمِرْتُ أَنْ أَكُونَ مِنَ ٱلْمُسْلِمِينَ ﴿٩١﴾ وَأَنْ أَتْلُوَا۟ ٱلْقُرْءَانَ

> And I am commanded to be from among the Muslims (those who submit to Allāh in Islām) and to recite the Qur'ān.[2]

[1] Qur'ān 29:45

[2] Qur'ān 27:91

And the Prophet (ﷺ) said,

> "Read the Qur'ān, for it will come as an intercessor for its people (i.e. those who recite it and apply its precepts) on the Day of Judgement."[3]

The scholars give different interpretations regarding what it means to "desert the Qur'ān"; at any rate, the Muslim must stay away from any action that may be considered to mean that he has effectively abandoned the Qur'ān. Imām Ibn Kathīr said that Allāh (سبحانه وتعالى) informs us of what His Prophet Muḥammad (ﷺ) will say:

يَٰرَبِّ إِنَّ قَوْمِي ٱتَّخَذُواْ هَٰذَا ٱلْقُرْءَانَ مَهْجُورًا

> "O my Lord! Verily, my people deserted this Qur'ān (neither listened to it, nor acted on its laws and orders)."[4]

This is because the disbelievers neither listened nor paid attention to the Qur'ān; Allāh (سبحانه وتعالى) says:

وَقَالَ ٱلَّذِينَ كَفَرُواْ لَا تَسْمَعُواْ لِهَٰذَا ٱلْقُرْءَانِ
وَٱلْغَوْاْ فِيهِ لَعَلَّكُمْ تَغْلِبُونَ ٢٦

> And those who disbelieve say: "Listen not to this Qur'ān, and make noise in the midst of its (recitation) that you may overcome."[5]

When they were in hearing distance as the Qur'an was being recited, the disbelievers would speak loudly about other topics, drowning out its recitation: this is a form of deserting the Qur'ān. To not have faith in the Qur'ān is another means of deserting it. To not reflect on its meanings and precepts is also tantamount to deserting the Qur'ān. To spend all of one's time listening to song or to poetry or to other speech, and to not spend any time reading the Qur'ān – this is also a form of deserting the Qur'ān. And to abandon applying its precepts – by not following its commands

---

[3] Muslim (804).

[4] Qur'ān 25:30.

[5] Qur'ān 41:26.

and by transgressing its prohibitions – is another way of deserting the Qur'ān.

And guidance lies with Allāh (ﷻ). O Allāh, send prayers and salutations on Muḥammad, his family, and his companions.[6]

Listening to the News Instead of the Qur'ān

2-Q: When driving my car or sitting at home, I often listen to the recitation of the Qur'ān. Yet at times, one feels the need to listen to something else, such as the news; or to do something else, such as read the newspaper. I find that I have trouble organizing my spare time to do both: to listen to the Qur'ān and to perform other activities. My question is this: If I have a choice between listening to the Qur'an and hearing the news on the radio and if I then choose the latter option, have I in effect deserted the Qur'an and turned my back to it?

A: All praise is for Allāh alone, and may His prayers and salutations be on Muḥammad, his family, and his companions.

There is nothing wrong in listening to the news or in reading a newspaper rather than listening to the Qur'ān radio station – because for each there is a time. So by listening to the news, you are not turning your back on the Qur'ān so long as you allot time in your schedule for reciting and listening to the Qur'ān.

And guidance lies with Allāh (ﷻ). O Allāh, send prayers and salutations on Muḥammad, his family, and his companions.[7]

---

[6] *Fatāwa al-Lajnah al-Dāi'mah*, the third question from *Fatwa* # 6561; 'Abdul-Razzāq 'Afifi (Vice-President), 'Abdul-'Azīz ibn 'Abdullāh ibn Bāz (President).

[7] *Fatāwa al-Lajnah al-Dāi'mah*, the third question from *Fatwa* # 7108; 'Abdul-Razzāq 'Afifi (Vice-President), 'Abdul-'Azīz ibn 'Abdullāh ibn Bāz (President).

You Must not Stop Reciting the Qur'ān

3-Q: I know a man who used to be a student of the Qur'ān; however, he hasn't read it for an entire year now; what is the Islamic ruling regarding his situation?

A: All praise is for Allāh alone, and may His prayers and salutations be upon Muḥammad, his family, and his companions.

That should not be. Those who know him, especially those who have knowledge, should advise him and explain to him the virtues of reciting and contemplating the Qur'ān, and perhaps as a result, he may change and begin to recite and study it again.

And guidance lies with Allāh (سُبْحَانَهُ وَتَعَالَى). O Allāh, send prayers and salutations on Muḥammad, his family, and his companions.[8]

It is Recommended to Recite the Qur'ān Often

4-Q: Is reciting the Qur'ān wājib (compulsory) or mustaḥabb (recommended)? And what about abandoning it: is doing so Ḥarām (forbidden) or makrūh (hated but not forbidden)?

A: All praise is for Allāh alone, and may His prayers and salutations be upon Muḥammad, his family, and his companions.

First, Allāh (سُبْحَانَهُ وَتَعَالَى) revealed the Qur'ān so that people may believe in it, recite it, seek remedy with it from diseases of the heart, learn its precepts, and apply those precepts – both on an individual and a societal level.

There are different levels of "abandoning the Qur'ān." Some might disbelieve in it and not listen to it; others might believe

---

[8] *Fatāwa al-Lajnah al-Dāi'mah*, the third question from *Fatwa* # 7175; ʿAbdul-Razzāq ʿAfifi (Vice-President), ʿAbdul-ʿAzīz ibn ʿAbdullāh ibn Bāz (President).

in it, but at the same time do not study it; others might study it without reciting it; others might recite it without contemplating its meanings; others might recite it as a ritual without seeking from it a cure to the diseases in their hearts; and yet others might contemplate it without actually applying its precepts and without seeking to be guided by it in their conduct and in their societal laws. To the degree that one turns his back on the Qur'ān, one is considered to have "abandoned the Qur'ān."

Every Muslim must fear Allāh (ﷻ) and strive to seek benefit from the Qur'ān. And the more benefits one avoids achieving regarding the Qur'ān, the more will he be described as having abandoned the Qur'ān.

As for reciting the Qur'ān, it is not only legislated but it is also *mustaḥabb* (recommended, meaning that the person who does it will receive reward) to do so often, and – though not compulsory – to finish reading it once a month. And guidance lies with Allāh (ﷻ). O Allāh, send prayers and salutations on Muḥammad, his family, and his companions.[9]

If You are About to Recite the Qur'ān, then First Seek Refuge in Allāh From the Cursed *Shayṭān*

5-Q: Although I try to recite the Qur'an and although I love to do so, a feeling of constriction overcomes me when I sit down to read it, and I am not able to continue. What is the way out of my predicament?

A: The solution to your problem is given to you in this verse:

---

[9] *Fatāwa al-Lajnah al-Dāi'mah*, *Fatwa* # 8844; ʿAbdul-Razzāq ʿAfifi (Vice-President), ʿAbdul-ʿAzīz ibn ʿAbdullāh ibn Bāz (President).

فَإِذَا قَرَأْتَ ٱلْقُرْءَانَ
فَٱسْتَعِذْ بِٱللَّهِ مِنَ ٱلشَّيْطَٰنِ ٱلرَّجِيمِ ﴿٩٨﴾ إِنَّهُۥ لَيْسَ لَهُۥ سُلْطَٰنٌ
عَلَى ٱلَّذِينَ ءَامَنُوا۟ وَعَلَىٰ رَبِّهِمْ يَتَوَكَّلُونَ ﴿٩٩﴾ إِنَّمَا
سُلْطَٰنُهُۥ عَلَى ٱلَّذِينَ يَتَوَلَّوْنَهُۥ وَٱلَّذِينَ هُم بِهِۦ مُشْرِكُونَ

> So when you want to recite the Qur'ān, seek refuge with Allāh from *Shayṭān* (Satan) the outcast (the cursed one). Verily, he has no power over those who believe and put their trust only in their Lord. His power is only over those who obey and follow him (Satan), and those who join partners with Him (Allāh).[10]

Allāh (﷾) ordered us that, as we are about to recite the Qur'ān, we should seek refuge in Him from the cursed *Shayṭān*, and as a result, Allāh (﷾) banishes from us the presence of our unremitting enemy.

You must contemplate when you recite, for if you do so, your mind will remain concentrated, your heart will feel the positive effects of the Qur'ān, and you will be encouraged to continue. On the other hand, you shouldn't be concerned about when you will complete a chapter or a section; your sole intention should be to contemplate what you recite from Allāh's Book. The Messenger of Allāh (ﷺ) would read for long periods at a time during the night. When he read a verse that suggested meanings of mercy, he would ask from Allāh (﷾). And when he read a verse that mentioned punishment, he would seek refuge in Allāh (﷾). And this clearly shows that the Prophet (ﷺ) would not only recite the Qur'ān, but would also read it with an attentive heart and a reflective mind.[11]

---

[10] Qur'ān 16:98-100.

[11] *Fatāwā Al-Fawzān*.

To Memorize and then to Forget the Qur'ān

One Who Reads the Qur'an But is Not Able To Memorize It

6-Q: I read the Qur'ān but am not able to memorize it; will I be rewarded nonetheless?

A: All praise is for Allāh alone, and may His prayers and salutations be upon Muḥammad, his family, and his companions.

Even if one is not able to memorize the Qur'an, one is rewarded for reading, contemplating, and applying its verses. In a ḥadīth related by 'Ā'ishah (ﷺ), the Messenger of Allāh (ﷺ) said,

> "The person who is proficient in the Qur'ān is with the *Ṣafarah* (the Messengers or the angels), the *Kirām* (those that are close to Allāh (ﷻ)), and the *Bararah* (those that are obedient to Allāh (ﷻ)). As for the person who reads the Qur'ān, though it is difficult for him and though he stutters, he has two rewards."[12]

And guidance lies with Allāh (ﷻ). O Allāh, send prayers and salutations on Muḥammad, his family, and his companions.[13]

---

[12] Muslim [(898)-244].

[13] *Fatāwa al-Lajnah al-Dāi'mah*, the fourteenth question from *Fatwa* # 6292; 'Abdul-Razzāq 'Afifi (Vice-President), 'Abdul-'Azīz ibn 'Abdullāh ibn Bāz (President).

To Retain What You Memorized, Revise Often And Consistently

7-Q: What is the best way to maintain what I have already memorized from the Qur'ān?

A: All praise is for Allāh alone, and may His prayers and salutations be upon Muḥammad, his family, and his companions.

Constant repetition, truthfulness, sincerity, contemplation, a desire to keep what you memorized, an understanding of the Qur'ān, supplication to Allāh, ask of Him to grant you success in this regard, avoidance of sins, and repentance to Allāh (ﷻ) for past sins – by employing these means, you will be able – *Inshā-Allāh* – to maintain what you have memorized.

And success lies with Allāh (ﷻ). O Allāh, send prayers and salutations upon Muḥammad, his family, and his companions.[14]

Such a Person is Excused for not Having Memorized the Qur'ān

8-Q: What is the ruling regarding one who, though he reads the Qur'ān often, does not memorize it – not because of laziness or any other fault but because he has a very weak memory, so weak that it almost renders memorization impossible for him? And what is the ruling regarding one who memorized the Qur'ān but then forgot it, such as a student who memorizes verses or chapters for a test but then later forgets? Is there sin upon one who does this?

A: All praise is for Allāh alone, and may His prayers and salutations be upon Muḥammad, his family, and his companions.

---

[14] *Fatāwa al-Lajnah al-Dāi'mah*, the third question from *Fatwa* # 7349; 'Abdul-Razzāq 'Afifi (Vice-President), 'Abdul-'Azīz ibn 'Abdullāh ibn Bāz (President).

Whoever reads the Qur'ān often but cannot memorize it because of a weak memory will be rewarded for his reading of the Qur'ān and excused for not having memorized it, for Allāh (ﷻ) says:

فَٱتَّقُوا۟ ٱللَّهَ مَا ٱسْتَطَعْتُمْ

> So Keep your duty to Allāh and fear Him as much as you can.[15]

But if one memorizes the Qur'ān to prepare for an exam, for instance, but then later forgets it, then he has indeed done wrong and has indeed forsaken much good.

And success lies with Allāh (ﷻ). O Allāh, send prayers and salutations on Muḥammad, his family, and his companions.[16]

What is Meant by "Forgot" in this Verse?

9-Q: When I was a child, I memorized many chapters of the Qur'ān only to later forget them. Now that I am much older, I am trying very hard to regain what I had lost. However, up until now, I have not been able to recover those chapters that I forgot, and I fear Allāh's punishment, especially because of this verse:

قَالَ كَذَٰلِكَ أَتَتْكَ ءَايَٰتُنَا فَنَسِيتَهَا ۖ وَكَذَٰلِكَ ٱلْيَوْمَ تُنسَىٰ

> Allāh will say: "Like this, Our Āyāt came unto you, but you forgot them, and so this Day, you will be forgotten."[17]

---

[15] Qur'ān. 64:16

[16] *Fatāwa al-Lajnah al-Dāi'mah*, the seventh question from *Fatwa* # 7731; 'Abdul-Razzāq 'Afifi (Vice-President), 'Abdul-'Azīz ibn 'Abdullāh ibn Bāz (President).

[17] Qur'ān 20:126.

A: All praise is for Allāh alone, and may His prayers and salutations be upon Muḥammad, his family, and his companions.

Here, forgetting means to turn away from them and to not apply them.

And success lies with Allāh (ﷻ). O Allāh, send prayers and salutations on Muḥammad, his family, and his companions.[18]

Our Advice to Every Muslim: Train Your Children to Memorize the Qur'ān

10-Q: You obviously know and understand that the Qur'ān plays a vital role in the character of both a Muslim family and a Muslim society, so what advice can you give in this regard, especially considering that most Muslim families are neither trying to teach their children the Qur'ān nor making an effort to send them to circles of learning?

A: Questioner, you make an excellent point and what you said in the matter should suffice. The Qur'ān is indeed Allāh's Speech, and in reciting it there is great reward. The Prophet (ﷺ) said,

> "Whoever reads a letter of the Qur'ān, for him there is a *ḥasanah* (a good deed). And every *ḥasanah* is requited with ten of its kind. I do not say that *Alif-Lām-Mīm* is a letter, but *Alif* is a letter, *Lām* is a letter, and *Mīm* is a letter."[19]

---

[18] *Fatāwa al-Lajnah al-Dāi'mah*, the second question from *Fatwa* # 11469; ʿAbdul-Razzāq ʿAfifi (Vice-President), ʿAbdul-ʿAzīz ibn ʿAbdullāh ibn Bāz (President).

[19] Al-Tirmidhī, in a ḥadīth related by ʿAbdullāh ibn Masʿūd (2910). And Al-Tirmidhī said, "This ḥadīth is *Ḥasan Ṣaḥīḥ*." Al-Shaykh al-Albānī, in *Ṣaḥīḥ al-Jāmiʿ*, ruled that it is authentic (4/340).

In that case then, every Muslim must strive to recite and to study the Qur'ān, so that one may be from those who recite it correctly and properly; one should allocate a specific time during the day to recite the Qur'ān, so that not a day will pass without him reciting it. For example, one may assign the times after the Fajr and ʿIshā prayers to recite the Qur'ān, and if one establishes such a routine, then he should not abandon it altogether without substituting it with a new routine, for Allāh (سُبْحَانَهُ وَتَعَالَىٰ) censured those who abandon the Qur'ān:

وَقَالَ ٱلرَّسُولُ يَـٰرَبِّ إِنَّ قَوْمِى ٱتَّخَذُوا۟ هَـٰذَا ٱلْقُرْءَانَ مَهْجُورًا

> The Messenger (Muḥammad (ﷺ)) will say: "O my Lord! Verily, my people deserted this Qur'ān (neither listened to it, nor acted on its laws and orders).[20]

For one to desert the Qur'ān means that he turns away from it by not reciting it and not applying its precepts.

And we also advise everyone who is sincere to himself and who desires good for others to raise his children from the very beginning upon the memorization of Allāh's Book. A parent should encourage his children to love the Qur'ān while they are yet young, so that that love will remain with them as they grow up. In this country (i.e. Saudi Arabia) there are many schools; in every area, there is at least one school that is dedicated to teaching the Qur'ān. Children, in general, have free time at the end of the day, a time in which a parent should take his children to the said schools. Parents should encourage their children to study in them, even if by means of giving prizes for attending and for memorizing. The children will benefit others, by the will of Allāh (سُبْحَانَهُ وَتَعَالَىٰ), and they will also benefit their parents…[21]

---

[20] Qur'ān. 25:30

[21] *Majmūʿ Fatāwā wa-Rasā'il* of Shaykh Ibn Jibrīn.

You Should be Consistent With the Qur'ān

11-Q: I had previously memorized one-sixth of the Qur'ān, but then I later became so busy with my work that I stopped revising for a long time, and as a result I have forgotten everything. Am I sinning in this situation, and are there aḥadīth that contain warnings for people like me?

A: All praise is for Allāh alone, and may His prayers and salutations be upon Muḥammad, his family, and his companions.

I advise you to return to the Qur'ān – to recite it, to contemplate its meanings, and to apply its laws and commands. By becoming overly occupied in the affairs of this world, while being negligent in the affairs of your Religion, you place yourself in a dangerously precarious situation, whereby the end results of your imbalanced life may turn out to be evil. As for the ḥadīth that warns of an impending punishment for those who memorize and then forget the Qur'ān, it is a weak ḥadīth.

And success lies with Allāh (سبحانه وتعالى). O Allāh, send prayers and salutations on Muḥammad, his family, and his companions.[22]

In Order not to Forget the Qur'ān, You Must Assiduously Maintain it

12-Q: What is the ruling regarding one who commits the Qur'ān to memory but then later on forgets it? Will he be punished?

A: All praise is for Allāh alone, and may His prayers and salutations be upon Muḥammad, his family, and his companions.

---

[22] *Fatāwa al-Lajnah al-Dāi'mah*, the sixth question from *Fatwa* # 5168; ʿAbdul-Razzāq ʿAfifi (Vice-President), ʿAbdul-ʿAzīz ibn ʿAbdullāh ibn Bāz (President).

The Qur'ān is Allāh's Speech: it is the best of speech and it embodies laws and rules that govern all aspects of one's life. When you recite the Qur'ān, you are performing an act of worship to Allāh (ﷻ) – your heart becomes soft, and your soul becomes vigilant. For these and for other reasons, the Prophet (ﷺ) ordered us to maintain whatever we memorize from the Qur'ān:

> "Maintain the Qur'ān, for by He Who has my soul in His Hand, it escapes more easily than does a camel from its hobble."[23]

So the one who memorizes it should not be negligent, not in reciting it and not in revising it. One should designate a set portion of the Qur'ān for daily revision, so that he is prevented from forgetting and so that he may benefit from what he reads – commands, rulings, wisdom, etc. But if one forgets the Qur'ān not because he turned away from it or neglected it, but because – for instance – he became busy with life's exigencies, then there is no sin upon him. The ḥadīth that contains a warning to those who memorize and then forget the Qur'ān is weak.

And guidance lies with Allāh (ﷻ). O Allāh, send prayers and salutations on Muḥammad, his family, and his companions.[24]

We Advise You to Memorize it a Second Time

13-Q: I am now a young man 23 years of age, and when I was twelve years old, I used to go to a school to memorize the Qur'ān; at the end of my studies there, I had managed to commit the entire Qur'ān to memory. However, I have now forgotten most of what I had memorized – perhaps I have managed to retain

---

[23] Bukhārī, in a ḥadīth related by Abū Mūsa (رضي الله عنه) (5033); Muslim (791)-33/1.

[24] *Fatāwa al-Lajnah al-Dāi'mah*, the first question from *Fatwa* # 5169; ʿAbdul-Razzāq ʿAfīfī (Vice-President), ʿAbdul-ʿAzīz ibn ʿAbdullāh ibn Bāz (President).

only 4 parts of the Qur'ān out of a total of 30. Is there a sin upon me because of this? I have recently tried to memorize it again but I found it to be very difficult. What should I do? Should I try to memorize it again?

A: All praise is for Allāh alone, and may His prayers and salutations be upon Muḥammad, his family, and his companions.

We advise you to memorize the Qur'ān again for a second time and to be consistent in reading it, in revising what you previously memorized, and in applying what you know. We ask Allāh (ﷻ) to help us all and to make us successful. Nonetheless, there is no sin upon you *Inshā-Allāh*, for the *aḥadīth* that contain a warning to those who memorize and then forget the Qur'ān are weak, every one of them.

And success lies with Allāh (ﷻ). O Allāh, send prayers and salutations on Muḥammad, his family, and his companions.[25]

Is this Ḥadīth Authentic?

14-Q: The Prophet (ﷺ) is reported to have said, "The sins of my Nation were presented before me, and I saw no sin to be greater than that of a man who memorized a verse and then forgot it."[26]

A: I do not know of this ḥadīth; I have not read it anywhere. Nonetheless, there are two kinds of forgetting:

1) When one forgets because one is distracted or becomes sick: one who forgets for these reasons is not held accountable.

---

[25] *Fatāwa al-Lajnah al-Dāi'mah*, the second question from *Fatwa* # 9455; 'Abdul-Razzāq 'Afīfī (Vice-President), 'Abdul-'Azīz ibn 'Abdullāh ibn Bāz (President).

[26] Abū Dāwūd (461); Al-Tirmidhī (2917). Al-Tirmidhī followed Al-Bukhārī by proclaiming this ḥadīth to be weak.

2) When one forgets because one turns away from the Qur'ān and its recitation: such a person will be held accountable because his forgetfulness was a result of his negligence.[27]

Keep a Good Intention and Read the Qur'ān Often

15-Q: I have memorized two sections from the Qur'ān (from a total of thirty sections), but every time I memorize a chapter, I forget verses from the one I previously memorized. I seem to be afflicted with a disease that weakens my memory; please inform me of its cure, and may Allāh reward you well.

A: First, you must make your intention for memorizing the Qur'ān pure.

Second, you should recite the Qur'ān more often, for as the Messenger of Allāh (ﷺ) informed us, the Qur'ān requires from us that we assiduously maintain it because it escapes more easily from us than does the camel from its hobble. When you memorize a chapter of the Qur'ān, continue to repeat it over and over again, and don't move on to the next chapter unless the previous one is firmly cemented in your memory.

So again, make your intention pure and apply what Allāh (سبحانه وتعالى) teaches you:

وَاتَّقُوا اللَّهَ ۖ وَيُعَلِّمُكُمُ اللَّهُ ۗ

So be afraid of Allāh; and Allāh teaches you.[28]

And finally, do not move from one verse to the next or from one chapter to the next until what you have already memorized becomes firmly ingrained in your memory.[29]

---

[27] *Fatāwā al-Fawzān.*

[28] Qur'ān 2:282.

[29] *Fatāwā Al-Fawzān, Al-Muntaqā* (1/80,81).

In Order to Memorize, it is not Necessary to Read *Tafsīr*

16-Q: I try to memorize the Qur'ān, but I find that because of work, I am not able to read the Tafsīr (explanation) of the verses that I memorize. Should I continue to learn the Qur'ān by heart, even though I do not read the explanation of what I learn?

A: To read *Tafsīr* is not one of the requisites of memorizing the Qur'ān, so yes, you may do as you asked. But if someone is able to do both – memorize verses and study their meanings – then of course that is better. In your situation then, you can spend your time memorizing verses of the Qur'ān for now, and then later on, you can dedicate your time to reading *Tafsīr*. At any rate, whether you do one or both, it is not enough for you to study without practicing: you must apply the laws and commands of the Qur'ān.[30]

The Easiest Way to Memorize the Qur'ān

17-Q: What advice do you give to those who aspire to memorize Allāh's Book?

A: The Qur'ān has been made easy to memorize, for Allāh (سبحانه وتعالى) says:

وَلَقَدْ يَسَّرْنَا ٱلْقُرْءَانَ لِلذِّكْرِ فَهَلْ مِن مُّدَّكِرٍ

> And We have indeed made the Qur'ān easy to understand and remember, then is there any that will remember (or receive admonition)?[31]

What remains then is for one to be determined and to have a sincere intention. So if one is determined and if one finds pleasure in the Qur'ān, Allāh (سبحانه وتعالى) will make it easy for him to memorize.

---

[30] *Fatāwā Al-Fawzān – Nūrun 'Alad-Darb* – prepared by Fāyiz Mūsa Abū Shaykhah.

[31] Qur'ān 54:17.

There are, however, certain strategies that may help one to commit the Qur'ān to memory; for instance, one should assign a specific time during the day to sit in the Mosque with a Qur'ān teacher. *Alḥamdulillāh*, today there are many people who are qualified to teach the Qur'ān. In every area (of Saudi Arabia) you will find at least one school that is geared specifically to teaching people the Qur'ān; such schools provide excellent opportunities that weren't available only a few years ago. Young people should choose any gathering or any school, but what is important is that they should continue to attend until they finish memorizing the Qur'ān.

Just as important, or perhaps more important, than memorizing is to revise what one has already memorized, for a second time or a third time, and so on, until the verses become ingrained in one's memory. Also, you should apply the meanings of the verses that you study, which will help you to learn even more:

وَاتَّقُوا اللَّهَ وَيُعَلِّمُكُمُ اللَّهُ وَاللَّهُ بِكُلِّ شَيْءٍ عَلِيمٌ

So be afraid of Allāh; and Allāh teaches you. And Allāh (سبحانه وتعالى) is the All Knower of each and every thing.[32]

[32] Qur'ān 2:282

Issues Regarding the Recitation of the Qur'ān

Reciting the Qur'ān While Lying Down

18-Q: May I read the Qur'ān when I lie down on my side or on my back?

A: You may read the Qur'ān when you are standing, sitting, walking, jogging, riding a car, or lying down. Yet if you wish to fully benefit from your recitation, it is better to read when you are seated, facing the *Qiblah*: when you understand the meaning of the verses you are reciting and when you contemplate their meanings.[33]

Reciting as a Group

19-Q: When we are gathered in the Masjid, may we recite the Qur'ān in unison with others?

A: Your question is too general for me to give just one answer. If by your question, you mean that people recite verses as if they were one voice, each person in the group reciting in harmony with the others, all reciting each letter at exactly the same time, then it is a practice that is not allowed in the *Sharī'ah*, and at the very least, it is *Makrūh* (hated, though not *ḥarām*), because it is neither related from the Prophet (ﷺ) nor from his companions (رضي الله عنهم). If, on the other hand, you are referring to the same practice, but for the purpose of instruction and education, we hope that there is nothing wrong in that. And if, by your question, you mean people

[33] Al-Shaykh Ibn Jibrīn.

getting together to recite the Qur'ān, not as one voice, but each person at his own pace and rhythm, then it is a practice that Islām recommends, since the Messenger of Allāh (ﷺ) said,

> "No group of people gather in one of Allāh's houses to recite His book and to study it among them, except that tranquility descends upon them, mercy envelops them, the Angels surround them, and Allāh (ﷻ) mentions them to those that are with Him."[34]

To Make a Special Occasion Out of Finishing the Qur'ān, by Gathering with Others to Supplicate

20-Q: I noticed that when some brothers finish reading the Qur'ān, they gather with close ones to supplicate as a group, so that all may have a share in the reward for finishing the Qur'ān. In some such gatherings a special invocation that is related from Shaykhal-Islām Ibn Taymiyyah is spoken and sometimes other invocations are used. May one gather with his family and friends for this purpose? If yes, then is the permissibility in this issue limited to Ramaḍān only? Is such a gathering considered to be an innovation (bid'ah)? And is there a specific supplication that the Messenger of Allāh (ﷺ) would say when he would finish the Qur'ān?

A: We know of no specific supplication for this occasion, so one may supplicate as he pleases – by asking forgiveness for his sins, by asking for Paradise, by asking to be protected from the Fire, by asking to be blessed with an understanding of the Qur'ān, and so on. It is reported in an authentic narration that when 'Anas (رضي الله عنه) used to finish the Qur'ān, he would gather with his family to

---

[34] *Fatāwa al-Lajnah al-Dāi'mah*; 'Abdul-Razzāq 'Afifi (Vice-President), 'Abdul-'Aziz ibn 'Abdullāh ibn Bāz (President).

supplicate. Nonetheless, I know of nothing regarding this issue that is related from the Messenger of Allāh (ﷺ).

And I am not sure whether the invocation that is ascribed to Shaykh al-Islām Ibn Taymiyyah can be correctly attributed to him; at any rate, it is an invocation that is well-known and well-received among our scholars. And Allāh (ﷻ) knows best.[35]

If One Doesn't Understand the Qur'ān, is He Still Rewarded for Reciting it

21-Q: I recite the Qur'ān often; however, I don't understand its meanings; does Allāh (ﷻ) reward me nonetheless?

A: As Allāh (ﷻ) says, the Noble Qur'ān is full of blessings:

كِتَٰبٌ أَنزَلْنَٰهُ إِلَيْكَ مُبَٰرَكٌ لِّيَدَّبَّرُوٓا۟ ءَايَٰتِهِۦ وَلِيَتَذَكَّرَ أُو۟لُوا۟
ٱلْأَلْبَٰبِ ﴿٢٩﴾

> (This is) a Book (the Qur'ān) which we have sent down to you, full of blessings that they may ponder over its Verses, and that men of understanding may remember. (Qur'ān 38:29)

You are rewarded for reciting the Qur'ān, regardless of whether you understand what it is you are reading. Nonetheless, as a Muslim, you are required to apply the meanings of the Qur'ān, so it is not proper for you to be ignorant of its meanings, just as a medical student should not be ignorant of the meanings of what he reads in medical books; rather, the medical student works hard to understand what is in those books, so that he may then apply the knowledge he gains. The need of the believer to understand is even greater, for he recites Allāh's Book, which is a cure for what is in the hearts and an admonition for all people, which is why the Companions used to read only ten verses at a time, not proceeding

---

[35] Al-Shaykh Ibn Bāz.

to the following ten until they not only learned their meanings, but also applied them.

And my answer is yes, a person is rewarded for reciting the Qur'ān, regardless of whether he understands it or not. But you should strive as much as you can to learn its meanings, and to learn under the tutelage of trusted scholars. If you cannot find a scholar to learn from, you should read trusted books of *Tafsīr* – for example, *Tafsīr Ibn Jarīr al-Ṭabari* and *Tafsīr Ibn Kathīr*. And Allāh (سبحانه وتعالى) knows best.[36]

How Often should One Recite the Qur'ān

22-Q: Noble Shaykh, what advice do you give to someone who doesn't touch the Qur'ān for many months at a time, not because he has an excuse, but because he spends his time reading frivolous magazines?

A: A Muslim is required to not only read the Qur'ān often, but also to contemplate its meanings, which he may accomplish either by reading from the Qur'ān directly or by reciting from memory; Allāh (سبحانه وتعالى) says:

كِتَٰبٌ أَنزَلْنَٰهُ إِلَيْكَ مُبَٰرَكٌ لِّيَدَّبَّرُوٓا۟ ءَايَٰتِهِۦ وَلِيَتَذَكَّرَ أُو۟لُوا۟
ٱلْأَلْبَٰبِ ﴿٢٩﴾

> (This is) a Book (the Qur'ān) which we have sent down to you, full of blessings that they may ponder over its Verses, and that men of understanding may remember. (Qur'ān 38:29)

إِنَّ ٱلَّذِينَ يَتْلُونَ كِتَٰبَ ٱللَّهِ
وَأَقَامُوا۟ ٱلصَّلَوٰةَ وَأَنفَقُوا۟ مِمَّا رَزَقْنَٰهُمْ سِرًّا وَعَلَانِيَةً
يَرْجُونَ تِجَٰرَةً لَّن تَبُورَ ﴿٢٩﴾ لِيُوَفِّيَهُمْ أُجُورَهُمْ
وَيَزِيدَهُم مِّن فَضْلِهِۦٓ ۚ إِنَّهُۥ غَفُورٌ شَكُورٌ ﴿٣٠﴾

[36] Al-Shaykh Ibn al-'Uthaymīn.

> Verily, those who recite the Book of Allāh (this Qur'ān), and perform *al-Ṣalāt*, and spend (in charity) out of what we have provided for them, secretly and openly, hope for a (sure) trade gain that will never perish. That He may pay them their wages in full, and give them (even) more, out of his Grace. Verily! He is Oft-Forgiving, Most Ready to appreciate (good deeds and recompense). (Qur'ān 35: 29,30)

Recitation in this verse encompasses both recitation and following another person's recitation. The Messenger of Allāh (ﷺ) said, "Read the Qur'ān, for on the Day of Judgement, it will come as an intercessor for its people", (Muslim). And in another ḥadīth, the Prophet (ﷺ) said, "The best among you is he who learns the Qur'ān and then teaches it", (al-Bukharī). He (ﷺ) also said,

> "Whoever reads a letter from the Qur'ān, for him is a good deed, and a good deed is multiplied by ten. I don't say that *Alif-Lām-Mīm* is a letter, but that *Alif* is a letter, *Lām* is a letter, and *Mīm* is a letter."

And the Messenger of Allāh (ﷺ) said to ʿAbdullāh ibn ʿAmrun ibn Al-ʿĀṣ (رضي الله عنه),

> "Read the Qur'ān every month (i.e. finish reading it once a month)." ʿAbdullāh (رضي الله عنه) said, "I can handle more than that." He (ﷺ) said, "Then read it every seven days."

The Prophet's Companions used to finish the Qur'ān every seven days.

I advise all those who read the Qur'ān to read it often, to read it sincerely for Allāh (تعالى), to contemplate its meanings, to seek knowledge from it, and to finish reading it at least once every month, and if possible, in less than a month. If you are able, you may finish it in less than seven days, but it is better not to finish it in less than three days, because three days is the shortest period that the Prophet (ﷺ) recommended. Furthermore, to read the entire Qur'ān in less than three days might lead to a rushed reading, one that is without contemplation.

If you want to read directly from the Qur'ān, by touching it, you must be in a state of purity; if you want to read from memory, you do not have to first perform ablution. But if you are in the greater state of impurity (i.e. you have performed sexual intercourse or you have had a wet dream), you must first take a shower, both for reading while holding the Qur'ān and for reading from memory. 'Ali (رضي الله عنه) said, "Nothing would prevent the Messenger of Allāh (ﷺ) from the Qur'ān except for *Janābah* (i.e. the greater state of impurity)." (Aḥmad and the Compilers of the *Sunan*, with a chain that is *ḥasan*.) And guidance lies with Allāh (سبحانه وتعالى).[37]

"Chanting" the Qur'ān

23-Q: Noble Shaykh, in one ḥadīth, we are ordered to chant the Qur'ān – what does that mean?

A: Yes, we are encouraged to chant the Qur'ān, which means that we should beautify our voices when reciting, and not that we should sing. In an authentic ḥadīth, the Messenger of Allāh (ﷺ) said,

> "Allāh (سبحانه وتعالى) has not listened to something like His listening to His Prophet (ﷺ) reading the Qur'ān out loud and with a beautiful voice."

He (ﷺ) also said,

> "He is not from us who neither chants the Qur'ān nor chants it loudly."

In the first ḥadīth, Allāh (سبحانه وتعالى) listens, which is a quality just like all of Allāh's other perfect qualities, qualities that befit His greatness, and that are not similar to the qualities of His creation:

لَيْسَ كَمِثْلِهِۦ شَىْءٌ ۖ وَهُوَ ٱلسَّمِيعُ ٱلْبَصِيرُ

[37] Al-Shaykh Ibn Bāz

> There is nothing like unto Him, and He is the All Hearer, the All Seer. (Qur'ān 42:11)

What chanting means, then, is for you to recite out loud with a beautiful voice, so that your heart becomes moved, because the purpose here is to move your heart, until it is peaceful, until it benefits. The Messenger of Allāh (ﷺ) once passed by Abū Mūsa al-Ashʿarī, who was reciting the Qur'ān. The Prophet (ﷺ) stopped to listen and said, "Indeed, this one has been given a flute from the flutes of the family of Dāwūd." When Abū Mūsa (رضي الله عنه) approached the Prophet (ﷺ), the Prophet (ﷺ) repeated to him what he had said earlier, and Abū Mūsa (رضي الله عنه) said, "O Messenger of Allāh, had I known that you were listening to me, I would have adorned (my recitation) even further." What is important here is that the Prophet (ﷺ) did not then censure him for saying that, which was a silent approval from the Messenger of Allāh (ﷺ), indicating that it is recommended to beautify one's voice when reading the Qur'ān, allowing both the reader and the listener to spiritually benefit from the recitation.[38]

Kissing the Qur'ān

24-Q: When some Muslims are about to read the Qur'ān, they kiss it and then wipe it on their eyes and faces; is this practice correct?

A: I know of no precedent for this practice in our pure Sharīʿah.[39]

---

[38] Al-Shaykh Ibn Bāz.

[39] *Fatāwa al-Lajnah al-Dāi'mah*; ʿAbdul-Razzāq ʿAfīfī (Vice-President), ʿAbdul-ʿAzīz ibn ʿAbdullāh ibn Bāz (President).

“Allāh, the Almighty, Has Spoken the Truth”

25-Q: When I finish reading something from the Qur'ān, may I say, “Allāh, the Almighty, has spoken the truth (Ṣadaqallāhul-'Aẓīm)”?

A: Though this practice has become popular among Muslims, it has no precedent or basis or foundation in Islām; therefore you should not make it a habit or a ritual to say this phrase after reading the Qur'ān. The meaning of the following ḥadīth applies to the said practice:

> “Whoever does a deed that is not upon our affair, then it is rejected.”

Though we might not call this practice an innovation (*bid'ah*), it is nonetheless similar to an innovation. Some people go to further extremes, reciting this phrase during prayer.

To say, “Allāh, the Almighty has spoken the truth” after reciting the Qur'ān has not been related from the Prophet (ﷺ), his companions, or the pious early generations of Muslims. Just because this practice is now widespread, and because some people approve of it, doesn't mean that it is legitimate. If you read a verse of the Qur'ān that you are in awe of because of what the verse signifies in terms of profound meaning, you may, in such an instance, say, “Allāh, the Almighty, has spoken the truth.” But as far as we know, there is no basis for you to say it as a habit every time you read the Qur'ān: we arrived at this decision only after having researched the issue thoroughly and after having discussed it with the people of knowledge.[40]

[40] Al-Shaykh Ibn Bāz.

Stuttering When One Recites the Qur'ān

One Must Strive to Pronounce Each Letter Correctly

26-Q: What is the ruling concerning one who cannot pronounce the letter "Ḍād (ض)" correctly? Some people say that if one cannot pronounce this letter correctly, he should pronounce it as a "Tha"; others say that he should pronounce it as he does the "Dāl". What is the correct view in this matter?

A: All praise is for Allāh alone, and may His prayers and salutations be upon Muḥammad, his family, and his companions.

If one is not able to correctly pronounce the "*Ḍād*(ض)," then he should try his best and train his tongue to the utmost until he pronounces it properly. If, after having tried one's best, one is still not able to pronounce it correctly, then he is excused, and should pronounce it as best as he is able. Allāh (سُبْحَانَهُ وَتَعَالَىٰ) says:

لَا يُكَلِّفُ ٱللَّهُ نَفْسًا إِلَّا وُسْعَهَا

Allāh burdens not a person beyond his scope.[41]

وَمَا جَعَلَ عَلَيْكُمْ فِي ٱلدِّينِ مِنْ حَرَجٍ

And He has not laid upon you in religion any hardship.[42]

And success lies with Allāh (سُبْحَانَهُ وَتَعَالَىٰ). O Allāh, send prayers and salutations on Muḥammad, his family, and his companions.[43]

---

[41] Qur'ān 2:286.

[42] Qur'ān 22:78.

[43] *Fatāwa al-Lajnah al-Dāi'mah*, *Fatwa* # 511; 'Abdul-Razzāq 'Afifi (Vice-President).

You Must Strive to Improve your Recitation

27-Q: I am originally from Yemen and have been living in Saudi Arabia for the past ten years. I am an orphan, and from a very young age, I began to love reading the Qur'ān. Nowadays, I often read in the Mosque, but I mispronounce certain letters, which I ascribe to the fact that I have never studied in a school. Am I sinning because I make pronunciation mistakes when reading certain verses of the Qur'ān? Please clarify this issue for me.

A: All praise is for Allāh alone, and may His prayers and salutations be upon Muḥammad, his family, and his companions.

You must try to improve your recitation, and the way to do that is to recite often and to study under the tutelage of a learned and trustworthy reciter. When you will make a strong effort, Allāh (ﷻ) will make your affair easy for you. In an authentic ḥadīth, the Prophet (ﷺ) said,

> "The person who is proficient in the Qur'ān is with the *Ṣafarah* (the Messengers or the angels), the *Kirām* (those that are close to Allāh), and the *Bararah* (those that are obedient to Allāh). As for the person who reads the Qur'ān, though it is difficult for him and though he stutters, he has two rewards."[44]

And success lies with Allāh (ﷻ). O Allāh, send prayers and salutations on Muḥammad, his family, and his companions.[45]

Don't Correct Others While You are Praying

28-Q: This is what occurred in the Mosque: While a man was reading the Qur'ān and another was praying, the former made a

---

[44] Muslim [(898)-244].

[45] *Fatāwa al-Lajnah al-Dāi'mah*, the first question from *Fatwa* # 5948; 'Abdul-Razzāq 'Afifi (Vice-President), 'Abdul-'Azīz ibn 'Abdullāh ibn Bāz (President).

mistake in his recitation. The other man, while he was praying, noticed this and corrected him. I have two questions concerning this incident: First, is there a sin upon the man who was reciting incorrectly? And second, is the prayer of the other man correct?

A: All praise belongs to Allāh alone, and may His prayers and salutations be upon Muḥammad, his family, and his companions.

First, if the reciter was a beginner, one who was just starting to learn the Qur'ān and the pronunciation of different Arabic letters, then there is no sin upon him, for the Prophet (ﷺ) said,

> "The person who is proficient in the Qur'ān is with the *Ṣafarah* (the Messengers or the angels), the *Kirām* (those that are close to Allāh), and the *Bararah* (those that are obedient to Allāh). As for the person who reads the Qur'ān, though it is difficult for him and though he stutters, he has two rewards."[46]

Second, the person who was praying made a mistake when he corrected someone who wasn't leading him in prayer, but is excused because of his ignorance – thus his prayer was correct.

And success lies with Allāh (ﷻ). O Allāh, send prayers and salutations on Muḥammad, his family, and his companions.[47]

In this Instance, Your Mother is Excused Because She is Trying Her Best

29-Q: My mother is illiterate: she can neither read nor write; however – and thanks be to Allāh (ﷻ) – she fasts and prays. Because of her ignorance, she often makes mistakes in her recitation of the Qur'ān. Is there a sin upon her because of this

---

[46] Muslim [(898)-244].

[47] *Fatāwa al-Lajnah al-Dāi'mah*, the first question from *Fatwa* # 5948; 'Abdul-Razzāq 'Afifi (Vice-President), 'Abdul-'Azīz ibn 'Abdullāh ibn Bāz (President).

or is she excused? As much as I have tried to teach her the correct recitation, she still doesn't improve.

A: *Inshā-Allah*, your mother will not be held accountable for those mistakes, because she tries to the utmost of her abilities. The Prophet (ﷺ) said,

> "As for the person who reads the Qur'ān, though it is difficult for him and though he stutters, he has two rewards."[48]

As long as you continue to try to help her and educate her, you are doing well. Because she has tried and has been unsuccessful, there is no sin upon her – *Inshā-Allāh*. But she must continue to try – by studying with a teacher, by having others listen to her, and by listening to the recitation of the Qur'ān on audiotapes. When man makes an effort, Allāh (ﷻ) helps him.[49]

You Must Learn How to Recite the Qur'ān

30-Q: Though I read the Qur'ān often, I don't know the rules of recitation very well, and consequently, I make a lot of mistakes. Am I sinning because of this?

A: It is compulsory upon a Muslim to learn how to recite the Qur'ān, so that he will be able to read it as it is supposed to be read – as it was revealed to the Messenger of Allāh (ﷺ). One must try his utmost to improve in this regard, repeating one word at a time until he gets it right, and if then, he still makes a mistake, he will have two rewards from Allāh (ﷻ), for the Prophet (ﷺ) said,

> "As for the person who reads the Qur'ān, though it is difficult for him and though he stutters, he has two rewards."

So my advice to you, brother, is to learn slowly – studying one word at a time, even though it may be difficult for you – and to be

---

[48] Muslim [(898)-244].

[49] *Fatāwā Al-Fawzān, Al-Muntaqā* (1/81,82).

patient. If you apply this advice, your rewards will be increased. And beware of reading the Qur'ān in a hasty manner, not caring whether you are reading correctly or not, an attitude which indicates that you are taking Allāh's words lightly. It is strange that one of us should be negligent in this regard when we all know that the Qur'ān is Allāh's speech – He spoke it with the same letters and vowels that we use – which Jibrīl received from Allāh (ﷻ) and then delivered to the heart of the Prophet (ﷺ) exactly as he had received it. Allāh (ﷻ) says:

وَإِنَّهُۥ لَتَنزِيلُ رَبِّ ٱلْعَٰلَمِينَ ﴿١٩٢﴾ نَزَلَ بِهِ ٱلرُّوحُ
ٱلْأَمِينُ ﴿١٩٣﴾ عَلَىٰ قَلْبِكَ لِتَكُونَ مِنَ ٱلْمُنذِرِينَ ﴿١٩٤﴾ بِلِسَانٍ عَرَبِيٍّ
مُّبِينٍ ﴿١٩٥﴾

> And truly, this (the Qur'ān) is a revelation from the Lord of the *'Ālamīn* (mankind, jinns and all that exists), which the trustworthy *Rūḥ* [Jibrīl (Gabriel)] has brought down upon your heart (O Muḥammad (ﷺ)) that you may be (one) of the warners, in the plain Arabic language.[50]

And success lies with Allāh (ﷻ).[51]

Study the Rules of *Tajwīd* Under the Guidance of an Expert Reciter

31-Q: How should I go about learning the rules of Tajwīd (i.e. the rules of reciting the Qur'ān correctly)? In what book can I find the rules explained? I try listening to your Qur'ān radio station and I have purchased Hidāyat al-Mustafīd, but without benefit: because the book was not written clearly, I was not able

[50] Qur'ān 26:192-195.

[51] *Fatāwā Al-Fawzān – Nūrun 'Alad-Darb* – prepared by Fāyiz Mūsa Abū Shaykhah.

to understand it. I have also studied in Islamic schools here in Djibouti but also, to no avail. Please advise me as to how I can learn the rules of Qur'ānic recitation?

A: All praise is for Allāh (ﷻ) alone, and may His prayers and salutations be upon Muḥammad, his family, and his companions.

You can learn the rules of *Tajwīd* by doing the following:

1) Read about the rules of *Tajwīd* in the book you mentioned or in any other book that contains similar information.
2) Learn to recite the Qur'ān under the guidance of a proficient reciter.
3) On a practical level, recite the Qur'ān often; recite verses over and over again until you read them correctly.
4) Listen to the Qur'ān radio station (which is broadcast in Saudi Arabia).

And success lies with Allāh (ﷻ). O Allāh, send prayers and salutations on Muḥammad, his family, and his companions.[52]

Praying Behind Someone Who Recites Incorrectly

32-Q: What is the status of one's prayer when one prays behind an Imām who recites incorrectly, sometimes adding and sometimes decreasing the letters of the Qur'ān?

A: If the Imām's mistake does not change the meaning of the Qur'ān, then there is nothing wrong in praying behind him. For example, if instead of reading *"Rabbil"* in *Alḥamdulillāhi Rabbil-'Ālamīn*, he reads *"Rabbal"* or *"Rabbul,"* the meaning does not

[52] *Fatāwa al-Lajnah al-Dāi'mah*, the second question from *Fatwa* # 9566; 'Abdul-Razzāq 'Afifi (Vice-President), 'Abdul-'Azīz ibn 'Abdullāh ibn Bāz (President).

change, even though he read it incorrectly. If, however, he changes the meaning of what he is reciting, and even after being corrected he doesn't get it right, then one should not pray behind him…

During the prayer, if he is corrected, and if he then reads it properly, both his prayer and his recitation are correct. It is the duty of a Muslim to teach his brother, both inside and outside of the prayer, because Muslims are brothers unto one another: If one of them has knowledge, he teaches another who is ignorant.[53]

33-Q: I am the Imām of a Masjid in one of the neighbourhoods of Riyadh. My problem is that even though I have memorized at least three parts of the Qur'ān, my recitation is weak, which leads to a lot of errors during prayer. I am afraid that I am not able to bear this responsibility: should I continue as Imām or should I resign?

A: When you are learning to read the Qur'ān, you should strive to recite it properly. And I give you glad tidings that, if your intention is sincere and if you strive to improve, Allāh (ﷻ) will help you, for He (ﷻ) says:

وَمَن يَتَّقِ ٱللَّهَ يَجْعَل لَّهُۥ مِنْ أَمْرِهِۦ يُسْرًا

> And whosoever fears Allāh, and Keep his duty to Him, He will make his matter easy for him.[54]

And the Messenger of Allāh (ﷺ) said,

> "The person who is proficient in the Qur'ān is with the *Ṣafarah* (the Messengers or the angels), the *Kirām* (those that are close to Allāh), and the *Bararah* (those that are obedient to Allāh). As for the person who reads the Qur'ān, though it is difficult for him and though he stutters, he has two rewards."

---

[53] *Fatāwā Ibn Bāz – Kitāb-Al-Daʿwah* (1/57).

[54] Qur'ān 65:4.

I don't advise you to resign but I do advise you to continually strive to improve, seeking help through patience, until you not only finish memorizing the Qur'ān in its entirety – or at least mostly – but also learn to recite it correctly. May Allāh grant you success and make your affair easy for you.[55]

[55] *Fatāwā Ibn Bāz – Kitāb-Al-Daʿwah* (1/56).

Hanging up on a Wall a Poster which Contains Verses of the Qur'ān and other Similar Issues

Writing Out Verses on a Poster and then Hanging it up on a Wall

34-Q: As of late, more and more people are buying posters that display a picture of the Ka'bah or verses of the Qur'ān, posters that encourage people to be more religious. Many homes are now adorned with such posters. I have heard, though, that customs officials, by dint of an order from the Office of Religious Guidance, seize such posters. How perfect Allāh is! How is it possible that they let in dirty pictures, pictures that fill up our markets, while they forbid something so innocent? I feel that their priorities are not correct, which is why I hope that the respected office rectifies what has happened. And may Allāh (ﷻ) preserve and protect you.

A: All praise is for Allāh alone, and may His prayers and salutations be upon Muḥammad, his family, and his companions.

First, Allāh (ﷻ) revealed the Qur'ān as a reminder, as a cure for what is in the hearts of men, and as a mercy and guidance for the believers. For someone who has been blessed to appreciate the Qur'ān, to believe in it, to recite it, to study it, and to apply it – it serves as a light and will later on be a proof in his favour. On the other hand, the Qur'ān was not revealed so that it could be hung up on walls to beautify them; nor was it revealed so that it can be kept in special places, to act as a charm, protecting people from evil. Such beliefs are widespread among the common lot, and especially so among the innovators, who unfortunately, are many in number.

When one recites the Qur'ān, benefiting from it according to the purpose for which it was revealed, one is upon a clear way of guidance from his Lord. When one hangs verses up on a wall to beautify a room or to protect a house and its inhabitants from evil, then he has distorted the purpose for which the Qur'ān was revealed; he has strayed from the straight path and has innovated in the religion that which neither Allāh (ﷻ) nor His Messenger (ﷺ) sanction or allow. He has introduced something that was not practiced by the rightly guided *Khalīfahs* or the Companions or the *Imāms* of guidance from the first three generations of Islām, those generations that the Prophet (ﷺ) described as being the best of generations.

One will find that when people keep the posters referred to, they mishandle them when moving from one house to another. Or when the posters become old, they throw them away or put them in places that are not clean. It is the responsibility of every Muslim to venerate the Qur'ān and to honor its inviolability, and not to treat it in a way that is tantamount to debasement.

Second, this council has seen the three most widespread of posters. On the first is written "*Bismillāh*," and then:

فَوَلِّ وَجْهَكَ شَطْرَ ٱلْمَسْجِدِ ٱلْحَرَامِ

> Turn your face in the direction of *Masjid-Al-Ḥarām* (at *Makkah*).[56]

رَبِّ أَوْزِعْنِىٓ أَنْ أَشْكُرَ
نِعْمَتَكَ ٱلَّتِىٓ أَنْعَمْتَ عَلَىَّ وَعَلَىٰ وَٰلِدَىَّ وَأَنْ أَعْمَلَ صَٰلِحًا
تَرْضَىٰهُ وَأَدْخِلْنِى بِرَحْمَتِكَ فِى عِبَادِكَ ٱلصَّٰلِحِينَ

---

[56] Qur'ān 2:149.

> "My Lord! Inspire and bestow upon me the power and ability that I may be grateful for Your Favours which You have bestowed upon me and on my parents, and that I may do righteous good deeds that will please You, and admit me by Your Mercy among Your righteous slaves."[57]

Underneath these verses there is a picture of men and women making circuits around the *Ka'bah*. On the second poster, the "*Bismillāh*" is followed by the Opening chapter of the Qur'ān, supplications, Allāh's name, the Prophet's name, the names of the rightly guided *Khalīfahs*, and a picture of the Aqṣā Mosque.

To further clarify this issue, here are a number of reasons why it is not permitted to hang up the aforementioned posters in homes, schools, clubs, or places of business, regardless whether it is done for aesthetic purposes or simply as a charm, to bring good and ward off evil:

a) To use the Qur'ān in this way is to use it for a purpose other than the purpose for which it was revealed : it was revealed as a guidance and a good admonition that is to be recited.

b) Such a practice is contrary to the way of the Messenger of Allāh (ﷺ) and his rightly guided *Khalīfahs*. They followed no such practice, and we should know that all good is in following them, and not in following innovations.

c) It is *shirk* to believe in the power of charms. Though it may not be that everyone who hangs up such posters does so thinking that they are charms, it is a practice that may lead to that belief. Without a doubt, many people may become beguiled into thinking that by hanging up posters of the Qur'ān, they are protecting themselves and their loved ones. When one asks people who hang up such posters why they do it, many will say that they do so to bring blessings into their homes and at the same time to ward off evil.

---

[57] Qur'ān 27:19.

d) The prices of posters are raised when they have verses of the Qur'ān printed on them, but it is still a small price, since the Qur'an was not revealed as a means of providing business and as something to be marketed. The Qur'ān must be raised above such petty, worldly pursuits.

e) The spreading of these posters may lead to the debasement of the Qur'ān. Many people do not handle the posters correctly, dumping them in the garbage or a dirty place when they move from one house to another or when the posters become old.

f) In general, we must always strive to close any door that leads to evil, which was the way of the first generation of Muslims: thus the Companions were protected in their beliefs and actions from innovations, innovations that lead to much evil.

Third, we are not allowed to invite others to good by means of innovations, which may lead to evil, to *shirk*, to the debasement of the Qur'ān – especially when those means are in the interests of those who seek to gain material profits. The one who calls others to good has at his disposal many legitimate means of spreading the message.

Fourth, that many people have such posters in their homes and that such posters are prevalent in the marketplace are not indicative of them being permissible: the innovators and those who defend innovations outnumber those who follow the Sunnah (And there is neither might nor power except with Allāh). And because some people apply innovations such as the one in question, it is the responsibility of the scholars to point out those evils and to quell them.

Hence those from the Office of Religious Guidance who issued the order did what they were supposed to do, and may Allāh (ﷻ) reward them for their efforts. And because they are not able to prevent other evils, evils such as those you mentioned, they do not become from those who distort priorities: just like others, they can only prevent evil based on their knowledge and ability (i.e. maybe they don't have the ability because their powers of authority, as mere public workers, are very limited). So the good that they do perform for this nation is commendable and shows that they are performing the duties that are assigned to them.

And success lies with Allāh (ﷻ). O Allāh, send prayers and salutations on Muḥammad, his family, and his companions.[58]

Hanging Up Posters of the Qur'ān on a Wall

35: I praise Allāh with many praises, as He as ordered us to do. And I thank Him, for He (ﷻ) has proclaimed an increase for those who are thankful. I bear witness that none has the right to be worshipped except Him alone, and though the disbelievers and polytheists may hate it, that He has no partner. And I bear witness that Muḥammad is His slave and Messenger, the leader of mankind, whose intercession will be accepted on the Day of Gathering. O Allāh, send prayers and salutations on Muḥammad, his family, his companions, and their companions.

There are two matters relating to the Qur'ān that I wish to point out:

1) Many people hang up verses of the Qur'ān on walls – of whatever room it may be that they sit in. This practice is considered to be an innovation: it has neither been related from the Companions nor from the *Tābiʿīn* (Those pious Muslims who met with the Prophet's companions).

   The very reason why people hang up verses of the Qur'ān is unknown to me. Do they do so to glorify the Qur'ān? It cannot be so, for they do not venerate the Qur'ān more so than the Prophet's companions and the *Tābiʿīn*, and it has not been

[58] *Fatāwa al-Lajnah al-Dāi'mah*, *Fatwa* # 2078; ʿAbdul-Razzāq ʿAfīfī (Vice-President), ʿAbdul-ʿAzīz ibn ʿAbdullāh ibn Bāz (President).

related that these two latter groups ever hung up parts of the written Qur'ān on a wall.

Do they hang up verses of the Qur'ān to ward off evil? Well, it is not a correct way to ward off evil; if one wishes to ward off evil, one should read those invocations that have been related in the Sunnah for that very purpose, invocations that one doesn't hang on the wall, but utters with his tongue. The Prophet (ﷺ) said,

> "Whoever reads *Āyat al-Kursī* in the night, then until the morning, he will continue to have a protector from Allāh, and no *Shayṭān* (devil) will come near him."[59]

And this is *Āyat al-Kursī*:

ٱللَّهُ لَآ إِلَٰهَ إِلَّا هُوَ
ٱلۡحَيُّ ٱلۡقَيُّومُۚ لَا تَأۡخُذُهُۥ سِنَةٞ وَلَا نَوۡمٞۚ لَّهُۥ مَا فِي ٱلسَّمَٰوَٰتِ وَمَا
فِي ٱلۡأَرۡضِۗ مَن ذَا ٱلَّذِي يَشۡفَعُ عِندَهُۥٓ إِلَّا بِإِذۡنِهِۦۚ يَعۡلَمُ مَا بَيۡنَ
أَيۡدِيهِمۡ وَمَا خَلۡفَهُمۡۖ وَلَا يُحِيطُونَ بِشَيۡءٖ مِّنۡ عِلۡمِهِۦٓ إِلَّا بِمَا
شَآءَۚ وَسِعَ كُرۡسِيُّهُ ٱلسَّمَٰوَٰتِ وَٱلۡأَرۡضَۖ وَلَا يَـُٔودُهُۥ حِفۡظُهُمَاۚ
وَهُوَ ٱلۡعَلِيُّ ٱلۡعَظِيمُ ٢٥٥

> Allāh! *La ilāha illa Huwa* (none has the right to be worshiped but He), the Ever living, the One who sustains and protects all that exist. Neither slumber, nor sleep overtakes Him. To Him belongs whatever is in the Heavens and whatever is on the earth. Who is he that can intercede with Him except with His permission? He knows what happens to them (his creatures) in this world, and what will happen to them in the Hereafter. And they will never encompass anything of His knowledge except that which He wills. His *Kursī* extends

[59] Al-Bukhārī in a ḥadīth related by Abū Hurayrah, 2311.

over the heavens and the earth, and He feels no fatigue in guarding and preserving them. And He is the Most High, the Most Great.[60]

But to hang up this verse, as opposed to reciting it, provides no benefit whatsoever to the doer.

Do they seek blessings by hanging up parts of the Qur'ān on one of the walls of their home or office? By seeking blessings from the Qur'ān in this way, one is doing something that isn't legislated in Islām, something that is an innovation, and the Prophet (ﷺ) said,

"Every innovation is a misguidance."

Do they want to remind people – when they lift their heads – about a specific verse from the Qur'ān? But if one observes what actually happens, one will find that it has no effect. During a gathering, no one raises his head to read the verse or to contemplate the wisdom and lessons contained therein. (In a related issue, the pious early generation of Muslims disagreed: is it permissible for a physically or mentally sick patient to hang on his chest or to put under his pillow certain verses of the Qur'ān, to seek cure by such means. They disagreed because it is a method or a way that is not related from the Prophet (ﷺ).)

Or do they hang up verses of the Qur'ān for no particular reason other than as decoration, to make a wall in their house or office look nice. The Qur'ān was not meant to serve as a decoration: the importance and status of the Qur'ān is much greater than to allow it to be used as a decoration piece on walls.

Also, there is another reason why verses of the Qur'ān should not be hung up on walls: because the rooms in which they are hung up may be places where people backbite, where

[60] Qur'ān 2:255.

people lie, and where people perpetrate evil deeds, and if any of these evils occur in a room whose walls are adorned with the Qur'ān, then the people who are responsible are in effect mocking Allāh's verses: Allāh's verses are above their heads, yet they are disobeying Him.

For the above-mentioned reasons, which indicate that it is not a proper practice, I advise all of our brothers who have hung up verses of the Qur'ān to take them down.

2) As for the second matter, I address myself to calligraphers, those who write or draw verses of the Qur'ān in a writing other than the 'Uthmānī writing (i.e. the writing of the Qur'ān)... Indeed it is not proper for the Qur'ān to be drawn in a way that shows the genius of the artist, nor should it be taken as a decoration piece – because the Qur'ān was not revealed for the purpose of decoration and design. Whoever has in his home such drawings should burn them or erase them, to protect the Qur'ān from being debased or from being taken lightly. It is true that the scholars disagree about whether it is permissible to write the Qur'ān in other than the 'Uthmānī writing (there are three opinions regarding this issue); however, engraving it or inscribing it (for use as decoration) is without a doubt *ḥarām*.

We must, brothers, venerate Allāh's Book, honour it, and use it for the purposes that it was revealed for: as an admonition, as guidance, as a mercy for the believers, and as a cure for what is in the hearts of men. Read here of the wisdom for which it was revealed:

كِتَٰبٌ أَنزَلْنَٰهُ إِلَيْكَ مُبَٰرَكٌ لِّيَدَّبَّرُوٓا۟ ءَايَٰتِهِۦ وَلِيَتَذَكَّرَ أُو۟لُوا۟
ٱلْأَلْبَٰبِ ﴿٢٩﴾

(This is) a Book (the Qur'ān), which We have sent down to, you, full of blessings that they may ponder over its Verses, and that men of understanding may remember.[61]

---

[61] Qur'ān 38:29.

The purpose for which it was revealed is not so that it may be hung up on walls, nor was it revealed so that it may be engraved or inscribed in wood or in any other material.

And know – may Allāh have mercy upon you – that the best of speech is Allāh's Book; the best guidance is the guidance of Muḥammad (ﷺ). And the most evil of affairs are newly introduced matters (in religion), for every newly introduced matter is an innovation (*bid'ah*), every innovation is misguidance, and every misguidance is in the Fire.[62]

It Was not a Practice of the Pious Muslims From the Early Centuries of Islām

36-Q: Is it permissible to hang up on a wall, either in my home or office, verses of the Qur'ān or invocations related from the Prophet (ﷺ)?

A: It was not a practice of the pious Muslims from the early centuries of Islām to hang up written or inscribed verses of the Qur'ān, sayings of the Prophet (ﷺ), or invocations related from the Prophet (ﷺ). They would, however, read and study these texts, applying them, venerating them, and writing them down, not on a wall, but in books to read.

It is forbidden to hang up religious texts on a wall, especially verses of the Qur'ān, because by putting them up, one consciously or unconsciously makes them vulnerable to debasement. The posters that they are written upon might fall to the ground, or they may be debased in another way. For the most part, people put up verses of the Qur'ān as a decoration piece. Those verses may even be written in a style that is forbidden: some go as far as to place the letters in such a way that they take the shape of an animal or

[62] A written speech given by Shaykh ibn Bāz, which he signed, and which is distributed.

of a lamp, all of which indicates frivolity, which is impermissible regarding the Qur'ān. Sometimes the Qur'ān is written in such a way that it cannot even be read, which shows that the intention of the engraver is to show his artistic talent – a form of frivolity that the Qur'ān should be protected from.

Inscribing Verses of the Qur'ān on Watches

37-Q: The Permanent Council For Islamic Research And Fatāwa received the following question from Prince Masharī ibn ʿAbdul-ʿAzīz, who serves as President of a large trading company. He asks regarding the new Qiblah watch, which has entered the Saudi market, and which helps Muslims in different lands to know the direction to pray in.

A: After having seen the watch, and after having noted that written on the watch is the *Bismillāh*, *Āyat al-Kursī*, *Allāhu akbar*, and the phrase of *Tawḥīd* in Arabic (*Lā ilāha illa Allāh Muḥammadur-Rasūlallāh*), the members of the Permanent Council have answered the following:

Allāh (سبحانه وتعالى) has revealed the Qur'ān so that people may worship Him by reciting it, by contemplating its meanings, by learning its commands and laws, and by applying its precepts. As such, it will serve as an admonition to them and a reminder, whereby their hearts will be softened and their breasts will find a cure from ignorance and misguidance; whereby their souls will be purified from the filth of doubt, disbelief, and disobedience.

Allāh (سبحانه وتعالى) has made the Qur'ān to serve as a guide and a mercy for those who open their hearts to it, for those who listen to it with a presence of mind. Allāh (سبحانه وتعالى) says:

يَٰٓأَيُّهَا ٱلنَّاسُ قَدۡ جَآءَتۡكُم مَّوۡعِظَةٞ
مِّن رَّبِّكُمۡ وَشِفَآءٞ لِّمَا فِي ٱلصُّدُورِ وَهُدٗى وَرَحۡمَةٞ لِّلۡمُؤۡمِنِينَ

O mankind! There has come to you a good advice from your Lord (i.e. the Qur'ān, ordering all that is good and forbidding all that is evil) and a healing for that (disease of ignorance, doubt, hypocrisy and differences, etc.) in your breasts, -a guidance and a mercy (explaining lawful and unlawful things, etc) for the believers.[63]

ٱللَّهُ نَزَّلَ أَحْسَنَ ٱلْحَدِيثِ كِتَـٰبًا مُّتَشَـٰبِهًا مَّثَانِىَ تَقْشَعِرُّ مِنْهُ
جُلُودُ ٱلَّذِينَ يَخْشَوْنَ رَبَّهُمْ ثُمَّ تَلِينُ جُلُودُهُمْ وَقُلُوبُهُمْ
إِلَىٰ ذِكْرِ ٱللَّهِ ۚ ذَٰلِكَ هُدَى ٱللَّهِ يَهْدِى بِهِۦ مَن يَشَآءُ

Allāh has sent down the best statement, a book (the Qur'ān), its parts resembling each other in goodness and truth, oft repeated. The skins of those who fear from their Lord shiver from it (when they recite it or hear it). Then their skin and their heart soften to the remembrance of Allāh. That is the guidance of Allāh. He guides therewith whom He pleases.[64]

إِنَّ فِى ذَٰلِكَ لَذِكْرَىٰ لِمَن كَانَ
لَهُۥ قَلْبٌ أَوْ أَلْقَى ٱلسَّمْعَ وَهُوَ شَهِيدٌ ﴿٣٧﴾

Verily, therein indeed a reminder for him who has a heart or gives ear while he is heedful.[65]

Allāh has sent down the Qur'ān as a miracle for His Messenger, Muḥammad (ﷺ), and as a wonderful sign to prove that he is indeed His Messenger, a Messenger to all people, bringing to them mercy and establishing upon them a proof, from which they have no excuse. Allāh (سُبْحَانَهُ وَتَعَالَىٰ) says:

وَقَالُوا۟ لَوْلَآ أُنزِلَ عَلَيْهِ
ءَايَـٰتٌ مِّن رَّبِّهِۦ ۖ قُلْ إِنَّمَا ٱلْـَٔايَـٰتُ عِندَ ٱللَّهِ وَإِنَّمَآ أَنَا۠ نَذِيرٌ
مُّبِينٌ ﴿٥٠﴾ أَوَلَمْ يَكْفِهِمْ أَنَّآ أَنزَلْنَا عَلَيْكَ ٱلْكِتَـٰبَ
يُتْلَىٰ عَلَيْهِمْ ۚ إِنَّ فِى ذَٰلِكَ لَرَحْمَةً وَذِكْرَىٰ لِقَوْمٍ
يُؤْمِنُونَ ﴿٥١﴾

[63] Qur'ān 10:57.

[64] Qur'ān 39:23.

[65] Qur'ān 50:37.

And they say: "Why are not signs sent down to him from his Lord? Say: the signs are only with Allāh and I am only a plain Warner." Is it not sufficient for them that We have sent down to you the Book (the Qur'ān) which is recited to them? Verily, herein is mercy and reminder (or an admonition) for a people who believe.[66]

تِلْكَ ءَايَٰتُ ٱلْكِتَٰبِ ٱلْمُبِينِ ۝٢

These are Verses of the manifest Book (that makes clear truth from falsehood, good from evil, etc.).[67]

تِلْكَ ءَايَٰتُ ٱلْكِتَٰبِ ٱلْحَكِيمِ ۝٢

These are the Verses of the Wise Book (the Qur'ān).[68]

Therefore the Qur'ān is a book of guidance, of laws, of moral lessons, and of a code for living; it is also a great miracle and an irrefutable proof with which Allāh (سبحانه وتعالى) helped His Messenger. What it is not is a decoration piece that is to be written on a watch, to be marketed and sold, nor are its verses to be written down and used as charms to ward off evil. When one writes the Qur'ān on a watch or on something similar, one deviates from the true purpose for which the Qur'ān was revealed; moreover, by wearing such a watch, one makes Allāh's verses vulnerable to debasement by taking it into filthy places, for instance, the washroom. It is a practice that is contrary to the guidance of the Messenger of Allāh (ﷺ), the guidance of his companions (رضي الله عنهم), and the guidance of those pious Muslims from the early centuries of Islām.

If one truly believes in the Qur'ān and the way of the Prophet (ﷺ), and if one wants good to befall him, then one should seek blessings in his religious and worldly affairs from Allāh (سبحانه وتعالى) by reciting Allāh's Book, by applying it both in his worship and in his

[66] Qur'ān 29:50,51.

[67] Qur'ān 28:2.

[68] Qur'ān 31:2.

dealings. When one does that, Allāh (ﷻ) will bless him, increase for him his reward, and protect him in every situation.

The same can be said for the phrases that are written on the screen of the watch: *Allāhu akbar, Lā ilāha illa Allāh, Muḥammadur-Rasūlallāh*. One speaks these phrases to glorify Allāh (ﷻ) and to praise Him; in fact, the first phrase is the key to entering Islām; it is the sign of faith, by which the blood and wealth of the person who speaks it are protected. The purpose of these phrases, then, is not to serve as an adornment, to make the watch look nicer. It is obvious that since the watches were manufactured to help people know the direction of the *Qiblah*, the writing down of the said verses and phrases is not a necessary part of fulfilling that purpose. Only as a marketing tool does the manufacturer inscribe them on the watch and then many consumers later on use them as a charm, to invite good and to ward off evil.

For the reasons mentioned above, our view is that, as long as they contain the said writings, the watches in question should not be imported. And guidance lies with Allāh (ﷻ). O Allāh, send prayers and salutations on Muḥammad, his family, and his companions.[69]

Inscribing Verses of the Qur'ān on Posters

38-Q: The world has advanced greatly in the realm of advertising and the spreading of information; in our own small way, as owners of a plastic factory, we have produced many items that should serve to remind people of Allāh (ﷻ), items on which are inscribed verses from the Qur'ān, sayings of the Prophet (ﷺ), and some of Allāh's most beautiful names. We have made these products in such a way as to make it near impossible to have them debased; they are shaped in a way that makes it impossible

---

[69] *Fatāwa al-Lajnah al-Dāi'mah*, *Fatwa* # 1683; ʿAbdul-Razzāq ʿAfifi (Vice-President), ʿAbdul-ʿAzīz ibn ʿAbdullāh ibn Bāz (President).

to use them as dishes for food or drink, and the material we use is so expensive that no one would consider throwing the product away. We have found that Christians spread their message in this way, by giving out stickers, posters, and plaques that are hung up in places of gathering. They want people to see their message wherever they go, so that it will become ingrained in their minds. Their message is one of disbelief, yet the methods they employ to spread that message are strong, which is why they are able to make so many people believe in falsehood. Muslims, then, have a greater right to remind people of Allāh (ﷻ), which is all the more reason why they should use all means at their disposal. Allāh (ﷻ) has blessed me, in that the products I sell contain Allāh's speech and the Prophet's sayings. They are products that are hung up high, in respectable, clean places, to remind people of their duty to their Lord:

فَذَكِّرْ بِالْقُرْءَانِ مَن يَخَافُ وَعِيدِ

But warn by the Qur'ān, him who fears My threat.[70]

And that is why I play my role in spreading Islamic thought, so that it may be raised above all other ways; and my success lies with Allāh (ﷻ).

A: All praise is for Allāh alone, and may His prayers and salutations be upon Muḥammad, his family, and his companions.

Allāh (ﷻ) revealed the Qur'ān, a Book that is meant to serve in different ways: An admonition and lesson to mankind; a cure for what is in the breasts of men, ranging from the disease of disbelief to that of sinning; a Book by which men are guided, both in their worship and in their dealings; and a book with which Allāh (ﷻ) shows mercy to his believing slaves, those who recite the Qur'ān correctly, those who seek guidance from it in all of their affairs, and those who apply it in all situations. Allāh (ﷻ) says:

[70] Qur'ān 50:45.

يَٰٓأَيُّهَا ٱلنَّاسُ قَدْ جَآءَتْكُم مَّوْعِظَةٌ مِّن رَّبِّكُمْ وَشِفَآءٌ لِّمَا فِى ٱلصُّدُورِ وَهُدًى وَرَحْمَةٌ لِّلْمُؤْمِنِينَ

O mankind! There has come to you a good advice from your Lord, and a healing for that (disease of ignorance, doubt, hypocrisy and differences, etc.) in your breasts, -a guidance and a mercy (explaining lawful and unlawful things, etc) for the believers.[71]

وَنُنَزِّلُ مِنَ ٱلْقُرْءَانِ مَا هُوَ شِفَآءٌ وَرَحْمَةٌ لِّلْمُؤْمِنِينَ ۙ وَلَا يَزِيدُ ٱلظَّٰلِمِينَ إِلَّا خَسَارًا ﴿٨٢﴾

And We sent from the Qur'ān that which is a healing and mercy to those who believe and it increases the *Ẓalimūn* (polytheists and wrong doers) in nothing but loss.[72]

قُلْ هُوَ لِلَّذِينَ ءَامَنُوا۟ هُدًى وَشِفَآءٌ ۖ وَٱلَّذِينَ لَا يُؤْمِنُونَ فِىٓ ءَاذَانِهِمْ وَقْرٌ وَهُوَ عَلَيْهِمْ عَمًى ۚ أُو۟لَٰٓئِكَ يُنَادَوْنَ مِن مَّكَانٍۭ بَعِيدٍ ﴿٤٤﴾

Say: "It is for those who believe, a guide and a healing. And as for those who disbelieve, there is heaviness (deafness) in their ears, and it (the Qur'ān) is blindness for them. They are those who are called from a place far away (so they neither listen, nor understand).[73]

The sayings of the Prophet (ﷺ) serve many of the same purposes, since they came as an explanation of the Qur'ān. The Prophet's sayings provide guidance to mankind, a detailed explanation of commands and laws, so that people may be better

[71] Qur'ān 10:57.

[72] Qur'ān 17:82.

[73] Qur'ān. 41:44

able to understand the verses of Allāh's book and to contemplate their meanings – perhaps that they may give thought:

وَأَنزَلْنَآ إِلَيْكَ
ٱلذِّكْرَ لِتُبَيِّنَ لِلنَّاسِ مَا نُزِّلَ إِلَيْهِمْ وَلَعَلَّهُمْ يَتَفَكَّرُونَ

> And We have also sent down to you (O Muḥammad (ﷺ)) the reminder and the advice (the Qur'ān), that you may explain clearly to men what is sent down to them and they may give thought.[74]

إِنَّآ أَنزَلْنَآ إِلَيْكَ ٱلْكِتَٰبَ بِٱلْحَقِّ لِتَحْكُمَ بَيْنَ
ٱلنَّاسِ بِمَآ أَرَىٰكَ ٱللَّهُ ۚ وَلَا تَكُن لِّلْخَآئِنِينَ خَصِيمًا ﴿١٠٥﴾

> Surely, We have sent down to you (O Muḥammad (ﷺ)) the Book (the Qur'ān) that you might judge between men by that which Allāh (سبحانه وتعالى) has shown you (i.e. has taught you by Divine Inspiration), so be not a pleader for the treacherous.[75]

And Allāh (سبحانه وتعالى) has named Himself with the most beautiful of names, so that His slaves may be acquainted with Him; so that they may believe in the perfection and greatness that those names signify; so that they may praise Him with beautiful praises; so that they may call out to Allāh (سبحانه وتعالى) by them when they are supplicating, both when they are afraid and when they are hopeful; and so that they may know those names, both in belief and in action, without straying from their intended meanings. Allāh (سبحانه وتعالى) says:

وَلِلَّهِ ٱلْأَسْمَآءُ ٱلْحُسْنَىٰ فَٱدْعُوهُ بِهَا ۖ وَذَرُوا۟ ٱلَّذِينَ يُلْحِدُونَ فِىٓ
أَسْمَٰٓئِهِۦ ۚ سَيُجْزَوْنَ مَا كَانُوا۟ يَعْمَلُونَ ﴿١٨٠﴾

> And (all) the Most Beautiful names belong to Allāh, so call on Him by them, and leave the company of those who belie or

---

[74] Qur'ān 16:44

[75] Qur'ān 4:105

> deny (or utter impious speech against) His Names. They will be requited for what they used to do.[76]

And the Messenger of Allāh (ﷺ) said,

> "Indeed Allāh (سبحانه وتعالى) has ninety-nine names; whoever enumerates them enters Paradise."[77]

Here, to "enumerate them" means to believe in them, to invoke Allāh (سبحانه وتعالى) by them, and to worship Allāh (سبحانه وتعالى) by their meanings and implications.

Allāh (سبحانه وتعالى) commanded us to convey to others the message of Islām, a task that the Messenger of Allāh (ﷺ) performed in both speech and in action. The Messenger of Allāh (ﷺ) would speak in front of his companions, exhorting and reminding them; he would write letters to kings and leaders, inviting them to the true Religion; and he would go to the gatherings of the disbelievers, conveying to them the Religion of Islām. But it is not known about him that he used to hang up on a wall a poster or a placard of any sort that contained verses from the Qur'ān, his own sayings, or one of Allāh's most beautiful names – nor that he would do that to decorate, to seek blessings, to remind others, or to give a moral lesson. The rightly-guided *Khalīfahs*, the rest of the companions, and those who followed them from the *Imāms* of our pious predecessors, those whom the Prophet (ﷺ) bore witness to as being the best of generations – all of these righteous believers followed the Prophet's guidance. They too, then, did not put up the said religious writings on posters or plaques or placards. Even after Islām spread throughout the lands, after books became widespread, and the means of communication increased, they would not put up such posters on walls. The early generation of

---

[76] Qur'ān 7:180

[77] Al-Tirmidhī (3507), who said, "This ḥadīth is *Gharīb*."; Ibn Ḥibbān related it in his *Ṣaḥīḥ* (2384); Al-Ḥākim, in *Al-Mustadraḳ* 1/16; Al-Bayhaqī in *Al-Sunan* (10/27).

pious Muslims understood Islām and its main teachings better than we do and they were more ardent in spreading it to the world. If the practice in question were indeed legislated, the Prophet (ﷺ)would have pointed it out to us and the companions along with those who followed them would have applied it.

Therefore one deviates from the true purpose of the abovementioned three – the Qur'ān, *aḥadīth*, and Allāh's most beautiful names – when one writes them on posters or plaques, to be seen and admired for their design, and to be sold and marketed for profit...Moreover, over a period of time, the poster is susceptible to decay or to neglect, especially when people move from one home to another or when people who are in a state of impurity touch and handle them. Also, it is forbidden to follow the disbelievers – whether Christian or otherwise – in anything that is contrary to Allāh's *Sharīʿah*.

Every Muslim must know and appreciate the Qur'ān's status, giving it its due right and fulfilling the purpose for which it was revealed. And let those beware whose practices are contrary to Islamic rules and laws: let them beware of a severe trial and punishment...

For the reasons just given, the Permanent Council for Islamic Research and *Fatāwa* takes the view that such posters, plaques, and the like should be forbidden from entering the kingdom. Similarly, it takes the view that no Muslim should be involved in the manufacture of those products – the inviolability of the Qur'ān, the *Sunnah*, and Allāh's names must be safeguarded.

And guidance lies with Allāh (ﷻ). O Allāh, send prayers and salutations on Muḥammad, his family, and his companions.[78]

---

[78] *Fatāwa al-Lajnah al-Dāi'mah*, *Fatwa* # 1706; ʿAbdul-Razzāq ʿAfifi (Vice-President), ʿAbdul-ʿAzīz ibn ʿAbdullāh ibn Bāz (President).

Writing "*Bismillāh*" at the Beginning of Every Letter

39-Q: The Minister of Health (in Saudi Arabia) sent the following question to the Council of Higher Scholars:

The President of the Committee for Islamic Awareness (From the Ministry of Ḥajj) sent me a letter in regard to prescription papers given by doctors to patients: at the top of each paper is written "Bismillāh-ir-Raḥmān-ir-Raḥīm." Because such paper ends up in the wastebasket, the esteemed President requested us not write the "Bismillāh" on them.

However, we feel that if that ruling applies to prescription letters, then it also extends to newspapers and magazines, which often contain verses of the Qur'ān, some of Allāh's names, or sayings of the Messenger of Allāh (ﷺ) – because they too, end up in the garbage can. Every publication that enters a home can easily come into the hands of children, who toy with them and then throw them in places that may not be clean and pure. The medical prescription, on the other hand, ends up with the Pharmacist, who can take it upon himself to keep all prescription letters and then to burn them. We ask you to give us the correct Islamic ruling in this issue, so that all can know its application.

A: Because of the proofs that indicate the virtues of writing the "*Bismillāh*," it is permissible to write it on top of the paper of a medical prescription. Indeed, the Messenger of Allāh (ﷺ) would write the "*Bismillāh*" at the beginning of all his letters.

Shaykh Muḥammad ibn Ibrāhīm issued the following *Fatāwa* in regard to this issue:

> Indeed, writing "*Bismillāh-ir-Raḥmān-ir-Raḥīm*" at the beginning of informative books and letters is legislated in Islām, for that was the practice of the Messenger of Allāh (ﷺ) in his letters. His *Khalīfahs* and his companions followed him and did the same, and the practice of writing the "*Bismillāh*"

at the beginning of letters and books continues until this day. Allāh (ﷻ) said:

وَأَلْزَمَهُمْ كَلِمَةَ ٱلتَّقْوَىٰ

And made them stick to the word of piety.[79]

Explaining this verse, *Al-Zuhri* said that the word of piety is "*Bismillāh-ir-Raḥmān-ir-Raḥīm*."

'Abdul-Qādir Al-Rahāwi related the following ḥadīth in *Al-Arba'īn*: Abū Hurayrah (رضي الله عنه) narrated that the Prophet (ﷺ) said,

"As for every matter of importance which does not begin with '*Bismillāh-ir-Raḥmān-ir-Raḥīm*,' it is cut off."[80]

Al-Khatib related a similar narration in his *Jāmi'*. We must venerate and handle properly any document that contains the "*Bismillāh*," any verse of the Qur'ān, or any saying of the Messenger of Allāh (ﷺ), for Allāh (سبحانه وتعالى) says:

وَمَن يُعَظِّمْ حُرُمَٰتِ ٱللَّهِ فَهُوَ خَيْرٌ لَّهُۥ

And whoever honors the sacred things of Allāh, then that is better for him with his Lord.[81]

Concerning the sacred things referred to in the verse, we must obey Allāh in what He has made compulsory and we must honour what Allāh has commanded us to honour: His Book and the *Sunnah* of the Messenger of Allāh (ﷺ), and the people of knowledge agree that the "*Bismillāh*" is part of a verse of the Qur'ān, in Sūrah Naml. And Allāh (سبحانه وتعالى) says:

ذَٰلِكَ وَمَن يُعَظِّمْ شَعَٰٓئِرَ ٱللَّهِ فَإِنَّهَا مِن تَقْوَى ٱلْقُلُوبِ

And whosoever honours the Symbols of Allāh then it is truly from the piety of the heart.[82]

---

[79] Qur'ān 48:26

[80] The *Takhrīj* of this ḥadīth can be found in *Kitāb Al-Adhkār* by Al-Nawawi, a book that has been commented upon by Bashīr Muḥammad 'Uyūn (p. 149).

[81] Qur'ān 22:30.

[82] Qur'ān 22:32.

What are the "Symbols"? They encompass everything which Allāh (سبحانه وتعالى) has commanded us about, which includes both Allāh's Book and the *Sunnah* of His Messenger (ﷺ). If one is finished with paper on which is written verses of the Qur'ān, and if need be, one may burn it. This is what 'Uthmān (رضي الله عنه) did: when he united the people on one copy of the Qur'ān, he burned all of the other copies, and the rest of the Prophet's companions agreed with him in this matter, so it is one upon which there is consensus. And if one sees someone doing something that involves the debasement of the Qur'ān, he must prevent him, if he can, for the Prophet (ﷺ) said,

"Whoever from you sees an evil, let him change it with his hand; if he is not able, then with his tongue; and if he is not able, then with his heart (by hating the evil), and this is the lowest level of *Īmān* (faith)."[83] And by the will of Allāh (سبحانه وتعالى), we will do what we have to do in this matter.

When paper on which is written the "*Bismillāh*" is thrown in filthy places along with the garbage, then the sin is not upon the person who wrote it, but upon the one who threw it away and belittled it.

And success lies with Allāh (سبحانه وتعالى). O Allāh, send prayers and salutations on Muḥammad, his family, and his companions.[84]

To Inscribe the Word "Allāh" on a Water-Cooler or Fridge

40-Q: All praise belongs to Allāh alone, and may His prayers and salutations be upon the last Prophet. The head of the Customs Office in Madinah asks regarding the ruling on water

---

[83] Muslim, in a ḥadīth related by Abū Sa'īd Al-Khudrī (رضي الله عنه), in the *Book of Īmān* (49)-78.

[84] *Fatāwa al-Lajnah al-Dāi'mah*, *Fatwa* # 2779; 'Abdul-Razzāq 'Afīfī (Vice-President), 'Abdul-'Azīz ibn 'Abdullāh ibn Bāz (President).

coolers in the Prophet's Mosque, because on them is written the word "Goot," a German word that means Allāh. He asks the Council what should be done about this matter.

A: After having studied the issue in question, the members of the Council gave the following answer: There is no harm in that, for a fridge is not a place where Allāh's name can be belittled; also, perhaps it indicates that the water put inside is donated in the way of Allāh (ﷻ), to visitors.

And success lies with Allāh (ﷻ). O Allāh, send prayers and salutations on Muḥammad, his family, and his companions.[85]

The Qur'ān is not to be Used for Base Purposes

41-Q: A dairy company here now sells cartons of milk, and on the cartons is written a verse of the Qur'ān:

لَّبَنًا خَالِصًا سَآئِغًا لِّلشَّـٰرِبِينَ

Pure milk; palatable to the drinkers.[86]

The end destination of these containers is garbage cans. If printing the verse on the container is Ḥarām and if throwing it away in the garbage is Ḥarām, please inform us, so that we can pass on the message to the owners of the dairy company. And May Allāh (ﷻ) preserve and protect you.

A: When the company you mentioned, and others like it, quote the Qur'ān or *Sunnah* in this fashion, they are not actually intending to quote a verse of the Qur'ān: they do not say, "Allāh says," or "The Messenger of Allāh (ﷺ) says." Rather because the situation is appropriate, they have used a verse of the Qur'ān to

---

[85] *Fatāwa al-Lajnah al-Dāi'mah*, *Fatwa #* 11018; ʿAbdul-Razzāq ʿAfifi (Vice-President), ʿAbdul-ʿAzīz ibn ʿAbdullāh ibn Bāz (President)

[86] Qur'ān 16:66.

sum up a message, or a slogan, if you will. This is more close to an allusion than it is to a quotation, because they have taken a verse from the Qur'ān and presented it in the form of normal prose, not in the form of a verse from the Qur'ān. Therefore, the rulings of the Qur'ān do not apply to it: an impure person may carry the said container and one who is *Junub* (in a state of major impurity, which usually results from having performed sexual intercourse) may read what is written on it. Nonetheless, it is not befitting for a Muslim to allude or refer to something from the Qur'ān or Sunnah when his motives are base or when he wishes to market a product, because an allusion to the Qur'ān in these instances amounts to a belittlement of the Qur'ān.

It is forbidden to throw written material – whether on paper or on cartons – into the garbage; the matter is much more severe when what is written is the Qur'ān. And if, by throwing away something that has the Qur'ān written on it, one intends to belittle the Qur'ān, then that is *Kufr* (disbelief).

And success lies with Allāh (ﷻ). O Allāh, send prayers and salutations on Muḥammad, his family, and his companions.[87]

Allāh's Name is Written on Some Prayer Rugs

42-Q: All praise is for Allāh alone, and may His prayers and salutations be upon the last Prophet, Muḥammad.

The Head of Customs sent this question to the Council of Higher Scholars:

Many different kinds of prayer rugs, of different shapes, designs, and sizes, enter into our country. Printed on some prayer rugs is Allāh's name or the name of the Messenger of Allāh (ﷺ)

[87] *Fatāwa al-Lajnah al-Dāi'mah*, *Fatwa* # 204; 'Abdul-Razzāq 'Afifi (Vice-President), 'Abdul-'Azīz ibn 'Abdullāh ibn Bāz (President).

– is this permissible? The businessmen who import these items argue that no debasement can occur, since such rugs are specialty items, to be hung on a wall and not placed on a floor.

A: It is not permissible to allow these items to enter the country because of the debasement that occurs when they are laid out on the floor and stepped upon. The argument that they are placed on a wall does not hold, since people will differ in how they use it: some may in fact hang it up on a wall but others will put it on the floor for prayer. One of the accepted rules in the *Sharīʿah* is that the door or way that leads to evil must be blocked.

And success lies with Allāh (ﷻ). O Allāh, send prayers and salutations on Muḥammad, his family, and his companions.[88]

[88] *Fatāwa al-Lajnah al-Dāi'mah*, *Fatwa* # 1614; ʿAbdul-Razzāq ʿAfifi (Vice-President), ʿAbdul-ʿAzīz ibn ʿAbdullāh ibn Bāz (President).

Books that Contain at Least Some Verses of the Qur'ān, and How Some Practices are Tantamount to Debasing the Qur'ān

Placing the Qur'ān on the Ground

43-Q: Sometimes, one finds it necessary, or at least convenient, to place the Qur'ān on the ground or on a prayer rug. Is it permissible to do this if the ground and rug are pure?

A: Since we must exalt the Qur'ān not only in a spiritual sense, but also in a physical sense, it is recommended to place the Qur'ān in a high place, for Allāh (ﷻ) says:

مَّرْفُوعَةٍ مُّطَهَّرَةٍۭ ﴿١٤﴾

Exalted (in dignity), purified. (Qur'ān 80:14)

If you need to put it down, at least try to put it down in a place that is slightly elevated; but if this is not easy for you, you can put it down on ground that is pure or on a carpet that is pure. Avoid placing the Qur'ān in a lowly place, on an impure surface, or on dirt, for by placing it in these places, you are debasing it.[89]

Resting One's Head on the Qur'ān

44-Q: In some Masjids, people lie down, resting their heads on the Qur'ān. What is the ruling regarding this?

---

[89] Al-Shaykh Ibn Jibrīn

A: Without a doubt, to use the Qur'ān as a pillow is not just *ḥarām*, but also a great sin. Muslims must protect the Qur'ān from all forms of debasement and from those who are ignorant about the inviolability of the Qur'ān; furthermore, mosques should be carefully guarded from such people.[90]

When Praying, Some Worshippers Have to Turn their Backs on the Qur'ān

45-Q: In certain Mosques, copies of the Qur'ān are placed between rows on shelves, and as a result, some people have to turn their backs on the Qur'ān; what is the ruling regarding this?

A: When doing so is necessary, we know of no violation being committed.[91]

To Store Personal Items Within the Pages of a Book that Contains Either Verses of the Qur'ān or *Aḥādīth*

46-Q: What is the ruling regarding one who stores valuables or other items within the pages of a book that contains verses of the Qur'ān or sayings of the Messenger of Allāh (ﷺ)? When admonished for having done that, one person defended himself, saying that he found no other place to store his things. Second, must I search through the streets, looking out for papers that others have thrown away, papers on which is written verses of the Qur'ān or aḥādīth? What can I do to alleviate this widespread evil?

---

[90] Al-Shaykh Ibn Jibrīn.

[91] Al-Shaykh Ibn Bāz.

A: All praise belongs to Allāh alone, and may His prayers and salutations be upon Muḥammad, his family, and his companions.

First, it is not permissible for a Muslim to store things or articles in between the covers or pages of a book that contains verses of the Qur'ān or sayings of the Messenger of Allāh (ﷺ); nor may he throw away – in the street or garbage – books that contain those two categories of writing, for doing so means to violate the inviolability of the Qur'ān and Sunnah, to belittle them. As for the first issue, one who claims that he finds only Islamic books to store his things in speaks an untruth – knowingly or unknowingly – for there are many ways to protect valuable possessions, enough to make it unnecessary to use books that contain verses of the Qur'ān, sayings of the Messenger of Allāh (ﷺ), or invocations that contain Allāh's name. In the end, the issue boils down to laziness and a weakness of faith.

Second, you may save yourself from sin and a guilty conscience by advising others not to use the aforementioned kind of books in ways that belittle Allāh's speech and not to throw them away in the street or garbage. You are not, however, required to, as a full-time volunteer, scour the streets, trying to gather written material that is thrown away; rather, you are required to pick up what is easy and what does not entail any hardship. And success lies with Allāh (سبحانه وتعالى).[92]

The Inviolability of the Qur'ān

47-Q: What is the Qur'ān's status in Islām?

A: The Qur'ān is Allāh's speech. He revealed it to His slave and Messenger, Muḥammad (ﷺ). He revealed it as a light and

[92] *Fatāwa al-Lajnah al-Dāi'mah*, first question from *Fatwa* # 6901; 'Abdul-Razzāq 'Afifi (Vice-President), 'Abdul-'Azīz ibn 'Abdullāh ibn Bāz (President).

guidance for mankind until the Day of Judgement. Allāh (ﷻ) has blessed some from the early generations of Muslims, as well as others from later generations, to memorize it, to apply it in every facet of life, and to return to it in all matters, both great and small. To this day, Allāh (ﷻ) has blessed some Muslims, Muslims who give the Qur'ān its full due, physically and spiritually. But regrettably, many are they who, though they call themselves Muslims, do not fulfill the rights of the Qur'ān and do not obey the Prophet (ﷺ); and I fear that the following may apply to them:

وَقَالَ ٱلرَّسُولُ
يَٰرَبِّ إِنَّ قَوْمِى ٱتَّخَذُوا۟ هَٰذَا ٱلْقُرْءَانَ مَهْجُورًا ﴿٣٠﴾

> And the Messenger (Muḥammad (ﷺ)) will say: "O my Lord! Verily, my people deserted this Qur'ān (neither listened to it, nor acted on its laws and orders).[93]

It is a clear fact that many have abandoned the Qur'ān: they neither recite it, nor reflect on its meanings, nor apply its precepts (And there is neither might nor power except with Allāh (ﷻ)).

Many Muslims have either forgotten or have feigned to forget that they must venerate the Qur'ān. In Muslim countries, many verses of the Qur'ān are printed in publications – newspapers, magazines, pamphlets, journals – yet after having read them, many people throw them into the garbage, where the Qur'ānic verses are blatantly belittled. Allāh (ﷻ) says of the Qur'ān:

وَإِنَّهُۥ لَقَسَمٌ لَّوْ تَعْلَمُونَ عَظِيمٌ ﴿٧٦﴾
إِنَّهُۥ لَقُرْءَانٌ كَرِيمٌ ﴿٧٧﴾ فِى كِتَٰبٍ مَّكْنُونٍ ﴿٧٨﴾
لَّا يَمَسُّهُۥٓ إِلَّا ٱلْمُطَهَّرُونَ ﴿٧٩﴾ تَنزِيلٌ مِّن رَّبِّ ٱلْعَٰلَمِينَ ﴿٨٠﴾

[93] Qur'ān 25:30.

> That (this) is indeed an honourable recital. In a book well-guarded (i.e. *Lawḥ-Al Maḥfūẓ*), which (none can touch but purified (i.e. the angels), a Revelation from the Lord of the worlds.[94]

Based on the meaning of this verse, and based on the view of the majority of scholars, one must be in a state of purity in order to touch the Qur'ān. In a ḥadīth related by ʿAmrun ibn Ḥazm (ﷺ), the Messenger of Allāh (ﷺ) wrote,

> "And only the pure may touch the Qur'ān."

In another narration, Ibn ʿUmar (ﷺ) related that the Messenger of Allāh (ﷺ) said,

> "Do not touch the Qur'ān unless you are pure."

And in yet another narration we learn that Saʿd (ﷺ) ordered his son to perform ablution before touching the Qur'ān. This shows the degree to which we must venerate the Qur'ān; then imagine those who use a newspaper – wherein the Qur'ān is written – as a tablecloth, throwing it into the garbage after their meal; without a doubt, by doing this they are debasing the Qur'ān. It is the responsibility of every Muslim to venerate the Qur'ān, books wherein verses of the Qur'ān are written, wherein the Prophet's sayings are printed, and wherein one of Allāh's beautiful names is mentioned; we can achieve a portion of that veneration when we store such books in a clean, pure place. If we no longer need pages on which the Qur'ān is written, we may bury them in pure soil or burn them. But we must not be negligent in this issue, feigning ignorance. We ask Allāh (ﷻ) to guide us to what He loves and to protect us both from the evils of our own selves and the evils of our deeds. We ask Him to put into our hearts veneration for both His Book and the way of His Prophet (ﷺ). We ask Allāh (ﷻ) to make us from those who follow these two noble sources, and from those who do not debase them by speech or by deed. Indeed, He is our Protector and is able to answer our prayers.[95]

---

[94] Qur'ān 56:76-80.

[95] This answer has been printed in the magazine "*Studies in Islam.*" (Vol.6, pp. 289-290).

It is not Permissible to Throw Newspapers Away into the Garbage

48-Q: In certain newspapers "Bismillāh-ir-Raḥmān-ir-Raḥīm" is written. The problem is that when some people finish reading a newspaper, they throw it away into the garbage or simply in the streets, while others use it for cleaning. What is the ruling regarding these situations?

A: All praise is for Allāh alone, and may His prayers and salutations be upon Muḥammad, his family, and his companions.

It is legislated in Islām to write "*Bismillāh-ir-Raḥmān-ir-Raḥīm*" at the beginning of informative books and letters; the Prophet (ﷺ) established this practice, and then the four rightly-guided *Khalīfahs* and the rest of the Companions followed him, and until today, when Muslims set out to write anything of significance, they begin by writing the "*Bismillāh*." It must also be said that it is a religious obligation to venerate and honor paper on which is written this phrase (or verses of the Qur'ān or sayings of the Prophet (ﷺ)), which is to say that it is forbidden to debase a sheet of paper on which is written the "*Bismillāh*," because it is a verse of the Qur'ān, and part of a verse in Sūrah al-Naml. Therefore it is forbidden to use such paper to clean, to put dishes of food on top of, or to wrap things in; likewise, it is forbidden to throw such paper into the garbage.

And success lies with Allāh (ﷻ). O Allāh, send prayers and salutations on Muḥammad, his family, and his companions.[96]

---

[96] *Fatāwa al-Lajnah al-Dāi'mah*: 'Abdul-Razzāq 'Afifi (Vice-President), 'Abdul-'Azīz ibn 'Abdullāh ibn Bāz (President).

It is Forbidden to Sell or to Give Your Newspapers to the Drycleaners

49-Q: After having read a newspaper, I store it away in a special room, and over time, I have accumulated a great deal of newspapers. May I give them away to someone who sells bread in the streets or to the drycleaner? The former uses newspapers to wrap bread in and the latter uses them to wrap clothes in.

A: It is forbidden for you to give your newspapers away to any of the two people you mentioned, because for the most part, newspapers contain Islamic columns, in which is written verses of the Qur'ān or sayings of the Messenger of Allāh or some of Allāh's most beautiful names. One must preserve such newspapers, and if one no longer needs them, he may either burn them or bury them in pure ground.

And success lies with Allāh (ﷻ). O Allāh, send prayers and salutations on Muḥammad, his family, and his companions.[97]

To Burn Newspapers and Magazines

50-Q: After having read newspapers, may we burn them? And if we find pages of the Qur'ān in the street, may we burn them as well?

A: All praise is for Allāh alone and may His prayers and salutations be upon Muḥammad, his family, and his companions.

Yes, to protect the dignity of those newspapers that contain verses of the Qur'ān or sayings of the Prophet (ﷺ), it is permissible to dispose of them properly by burning them. Similarly, to protect the Qur'ān from belittlement, it is permissible to burn its pages.

---

[97] *Fatāwa al-Lajnah al-Dāi'mah, Fatwa* # 3407; 'Abdul-Razzāq 'Afifi (Vice-President), 'Abdul-'Azīz ibn 'Abdullāh ibn Bāz (President).

Another way to protect the sanctity of the Qur'ān is to bury the pages you found in pure soil.

And success lies with Allāh (ﷻ). O Allah, send prayers and salutations on Muḥammad, his family, and his companions.[98]

Recycling Pages of the Qur'ān

51-Q: In many countries, waste paper is gathered and then recycled using chemicals and machines. Here in India, where Muslims and non-Muslims both live, non-Muslims run most recycling companies. When some Muslims finish reading a paper that contains verses of the Qur'ān or sayings of the Messenger of Allāh (ﷺ), they throw that paper away into large containers, which are then taken to recycling plants. Some Muslims say that this process involves the belittlement of the Qur'ān. Please clarify for us the Islamic ruling concerning this issue.

A: All praise is for Allāh alone, and may His prayers and salutations be upon Muḥammad, his family, and his companions.

First, it is compulsory to properly maintain papers on which is written the Qur'ān, for it is the speech of the Lord of all that exists; and it is forbidden to belittle it or to make it vulnerable to belittlement.

Second, it is forbidden to make it possible for the disbelievers to touch the Qur'ān.

Third, it is permissible for Muslims to properly and honorably dispose of such paper – either by burning it or by burying it under pure ground, so that it may be protected from harm and belittlement.

---

[98] *Fatāwa al-Lajnah al-Dāi'mah*, first question from *Fatwa* # 3916; 'Abdul-Razzāq 'Afifi (Vice-President), 'Abdul-'Azīz ibn 'Abdullāh ibn Bāz (President).

In regard to the issue of recycling, the members of the Council of Higher Scholars (in their 26th meeting) agreed that it is forbidden to recycle any paper on which is written the Qur'ān; this is what they answered:

1) What is done in terms of burning and then burying the ashes of such paper under pure ground is a good and acceptable practice: the scholars mention that it is good because by doing it, we follow the example of the rightly-guided *Khalifah*, 'Uthmān ibn 'Affān (رضي الله عنه).

2) The proposal of the Ghadīr Factory to recycle sanctified paper should be rejected, because it will involve belittlement and debasement of the Qur'ān.

3) Even books of ḥadīth, which contain the sayings of the Messenger of Allāh (ﷺ) must be well-maintained and protected from harm and debasement, and that can be achieved by burning such books or by burying them under pure ground.

And success lies with Allāh (سبحانه وتعالى). O Allāh, send prayers and salutation on Muḥammad, his family, and his companions.[99]

[99] *Fatāwa al-Lajnah al-Dāi'mah*, *Fatwa* # 9798; 'Abdul-Razzāq 'Afifi (Vice-President), 'Abdul-'Azīz ibn 'Abdullāh ibn Bāz (President)

Taking the Qur'ān into the Bathroom

Only When Necessary, you May Take it With You

52-Q: I Keep a copy of the Qur'ān with me in my pocket, and in the past, I may have inadvertently taken it with me when I went to the washroom. What is the ruling regarding this?

A: All praise is for Allāh, and may His prayers and peace be upon His Messenger, His Messenger's family, and His Messenger's companions.

It is permissible for you to keep the Qur'ān with you in your pocket; however, it is forbidden to take it into the washroom. We, as Muslims, must venerate Allāh's Book, and keeping it in a suitable place is one of the ways in which we venerate and honor it. But were you to fear, that by leaving the Qur'ān outside of the washroom someone may steal it (as sometimes is the case in public places), you may take it with you, because in that case doing so is a necessity.

And guidance lies with Allāh. O Allāh, send prayers and salutations on Muḥammad, his family, and his companions.[1]

[1] *Fatāwa al-Lajnah al-Dāi'mah*, the second question from *Fatwa* # 2245; 'Abdul-Razzāq 'Afifi (Vice-President), 'Abdul-'Azīz ibn 'Abdullāh ibn Bāz (President).

If You Forget, There is no Sin Upon You

53-Q: I carry the Qur'ān with me in my pocket, and on one occasion, I went to the washroom, forgetting that it was with me. What is the Islamic ruling regarding that mistake?

A: All praise is for Allāh, and may His prayers and peace be upon Muḥammad, his family, and his companions.

If in fact forgetfulness was the cause of the mistake, then there is no sin upon you. And guidance lies with Allāh. O Allāh, send prayers and salutations on Muḥammad, his family, and his companions.[2]

While in the Washroom, You are Not Permitted to Recite the Qur'ān

54-Q: I read the Qur'ān so much (Alḥamdulillāh) that sometimes I find myself, without realizing it, to be revising certain verses of the Qur'ān when I am in the washroom, verses that are often in my thoughts. What is the ruling regarding this?

A: The people of knowledge have mentioned that it is forbidden to recite the Qur'ān while one is seated and is in the process of relieving himself, because by reciting in the aforementioned state, one is belittling the Qur'ān. You must therefore be careful, by paying attention to what you say while you are in the washroom; don't let the *Shayṭān's* whispers goad you on until you give in and recite something from the Qur'ān. You should control yourself when you enter the toilet, being careful not to read anything from Allāh's Book.[3]

---

[2] *Fatāwa al-Lajnah al-Dāi'mah*, the fifth question from *Fatwa* # 10806; 'Abdul-Razzāq 'Afifi (Vice-President), 'Abdul-'Aziz ibn 'Abdullāh ibn Bāz (President).

[3] *Fatāwa Al-Fawzān: Nūrun 'Alad-Darb*. Prepared by Fāyiz Mūsa Abū-Shaykhah.

Using the Qur'ān in Normal Speech and in Joking

It is Advisable not to Replace Common Conversational Phrases with Verses of the Qur'ān

55-Q: What is the ruling regarding those who, whenever faced with a different situation in life, interpret the Qur'ān (to suit the occasion) and quote its verses? For example, when afflicted or when in a difficult situation, they may say,

تَؤُزُّهُمْ أَزًّا ﴿٨٣﴾

To push them to do evil.[4]

Upon meeting a companion, they say,

ثُمَّ جِئْتَ عَلَىٰ قَدَرٍ

Then did you come here as ordained.[5]

When a meal is served, they say,

كُلُوا وَاشْرَبُوا هَنِيئًا بِمَا أَسْلَفْتُمْ فِي الْأَيَّامِ الْخَالِيَةِ ﴿٢٤﴾

Eat and drink at ease for that which you have sent on before you in days past![6]

And there are even more verses of the Qur'ān that people use nowadays for various occassions.

A: All praise is for Allāh alone, and may His prayers and peace be upon His Messenger, His Messenger's family, and His Messenger's companions.

---

[4] Qur'ān 19:83.

[5] Qur'ān 20:40.

[6] Qur'ān 69:24.

It is advisable not to use such phrases during normal conversation. By avoiding this practice, we venerate the Qur'ān and guard it from that which is not appropriate.

And guidance lies with Allāh. O Allāh, send prayers and salutations on Muḥammad, his family, and his companions.[7]

It is Forbidden to Use Verses of the Qur'ān in Jest

56-Q: Is it permissible to joke with one's friends by quoting verses of Qur'ān, verses such as the following (For the first verse: when in a gathering among friends, and when someone present makes some kind of mistake, one might say jestingly,

خُذُوهُ فَغُلُّوهُ ﴿٣٠﴾

Seize him and fetter him.[8]

وَوُجُوهٌ يَوْمَئِذٍ عَلَيْهَا غَبَرَةٌ ﴿٤٠﴾

And other faces, that Day, will be dust-stained.[9]

سِيمَاهُمْ فِي وُجُوهِهِم

The mark of them is on their faces.[10]

A: All praise belongs to Allāh alone, and may His prayers and salutations be upon the Prophet, his family, and his companions.

When you quote a verse of the Qur'ān, it is forbidden to use it in jest. However, if there are certain phrases from the Qur'ān that

---

[7] *Fatāwa al-Lajnah al-Dāi'mah*, the first question from *Fatwa* # 3114; 'Abdul-Razzāq 'Afifi (Vice-President), 'Abdul-'Azīz ibn 'Abdullāh ibn Bāz (President).

[8] Qur'ān 69:30

[9] Qur'ān 80:40

[10] Qur'ān 48:29

are commonly used in speech, and if one is not purposely alluding to the verse that he happens to have spoken, then the action is permissible.

And guidance lies with Allāh (سبحانه وتعالى). O Allāh, send prayers and salutations on Muḥammad, his family, and his companions.[11]

Summing up a Moral by Quoting a Verse From the Qur'ān – Doing so is Permissible

57-Q: I often hear my Muslim brothers – when they argue to try to make a point – compress their view, mentioning a single all-embracing verse of the Qur'ān. Is this practice correct? And under what circumstances may one mention and repeat such verses? Here are two verses that are often quoted in this fashion:

لَّا يُسْمِنُ وَلَا يُغْنِي مِن جُوعٍ ﴿٧﴾

Which will neither nourish nor avail against hunger.[12]

مِنْهَا خَلَقْنَاكُمْ وَفِيهَا نُعِيدُكُمْ

Thereof (the earth) We created you, and into it We shall return you.[13]

A: If one's aim or point is correct, then yes, it is permissible to quote verses of the Qur'ān in the aforementioned fashion. So, for example, if something is truly bereft of benefit (physically and/or spiritually), one may say about it:

لَّا يُسْمِنُ وَلَا يُغْنِي مِن جُوعٍ ﴿٧﴾

Which will neither nourish nor avail against hunger.

---

[11] *Fatāwa al-Lajnah al-Dāi'mah*, the fourth question from *Fatwa* # 6252; 'Abdul-Razzāq 'Afīfī (Vice-President), 'Abdul-'Azīz ibn 'Abdullāh ibn Bāz (President).

[12] Qur'ān 88:7.

[13] Qur'ān 20:55

And if one wishes to remind others of man's relation to the earth – that man was indeed created from the earth, and will return to that earth, and then will be raised from that earth by Allāh (ﷻ) – then he may say:

مِنْهَا خَلَقْنَٰكُمْ وَفِيهَا نُعِيدُكُمْ

> Thereof (the earth) We created you, and into it We shall return you.

But if one quotes such verses, making fun of them and mocking them, then he has apostasized – he has taken himself outside of the fold of Islām. By making fun of the Qur'ān or of anything that is sanctified in Islām, one becomes an apostate, a ruling that is based on this verse:

قُلْ أَبِٱللَّهِ وَءَايَٰتِهِۦ
وَرَسُولِهِۦ كُنتُمْ تَسْتَهْزِءُونَ ﴿٦٥﴾ لَا تَعْتَذِرُوا۟ قَدْ كَفَرْتُم
بَعْدَ إِيمَٰنِكُمْ

> Say: "Was it at Allāh, and His *Āyāt* and His Messenger (ﷺ) that you were mocking?" Make no excuses; you have disbelieved after you had believed.[14]

In every way possible, we must venerate and honor the Qur'ān.[15]

It is Forbidden to Name Films After Verses of the Qur'ān

58-Q: What is the ruling regarding those in the film industry who name movies after verses of the Qur'ān, verses such as the following:

إِنَّ رَبَّكَ لَبِٱلْمِرْصَادِ ﴿١٤﴾

---

[14] Qur'ān 9:65.

[15] *Fatāwā al-Fawzān, Al-Muntaqā* (1:80,81).

Verily, your Lord is Ever Watchful (over them).[16]

وَبِٱلْوَٰلِدَيْنِ إِحْسَٰنًا

And be dutiful and good to parents.[17]

وَٱلَّيْلِ إِذَا سَجَىٰ ۝٢

And by the night when it is still (or darkens).[18]

A: All praise belongs to Allāh, and may his prayers and salutations be upon Muḥammad, his family, and his companions.

Because it debases the Qur'ān and confuses between good and evil, it is forbidden to name films after certain verses of the Qur'ān.

And guidance lies with Allāh. O Allāh, send prayers and salutations on Muḥammad, his family, and his companions.[19]

We Must Venerate Allāh's Speech

59-Q: Dr. Muḥammad Fatih asked the following question:

Here at the hospital, we have a very good phone system, one that allows the operator to go to another call, leaving the previous caller on hold. As callers are often put on hold, we decided to fill up that time by playing a recording of something religious, such as verses of the Qur'ān or sayings of the Prophet (ﷺ). Since some callers might not listen to what is played – occupying themselves during the waiting period with other matters – and since it might lead to the Qur'ān being neglected, we thought it better to seek your advice before programming religious recordings into the system.

---

[16] Qur'ān 89:14.

[17] Qur'ān 2:83.

[18] Qur'ān 93:2.

[19] *Fatāwa al-Lajnah al-Dāi'mah*, *Fatwa* # 8691; 'Abdul-Razzāq 'Afifi (Vice-President), 'Abdul-'Azīz ibn 'Abdullāh ibn Bāz (President).

A: First, I must point out that unless there is a necessity – an emergency arises or another call is more important or some other legitimate reason – it is not permissible to put people on hold because doing so involves harming others (i.e. by wasting their time).

Second, the Noble Qur'ān is Allāh's speech, which we must honor and venerate; we must not allow for common discourse and joking to be mixed with it, nor should we use it to fill up empty time as has been suggested by your question; rather, our first intention when reading the Qur'ān should be the worship of Allāh (ﷻ) and seeking closeness to Him – which we accomplish by contemplating the meanings and messages found therein. The same can be said for sayings of the Messenger of Allāh (ﷺ): we must not juxtapose joking or jesting with them. Rather, we should read them to understand the Islamic rulings that they impart and then to apply them.

And guidance lies with Allāh. O Allāh, send prayers and salutations on Muḥammad, his family, and his companions.[20]

---

[20] *Fatāwa al-Lajnah al-Dāi'mah*, *Fatwa* # 5959; 'Abdul-Razzāq 'Afīfī (Vice-President), 'Abdul-'Azīz ibn 'Abdullāh ibn Bāz (President).

Taking the Qur'ān to the Lands of the Disbelievers

It is Permissible to take the Qur'ān to the Lands of the Disbelievers

60-Q: When traveling to a land of disbelievers, may I take the Qur'ān with me?

A: All praise is for Allāh alone, and may his prayers and salutations be upon Muḥammad, his family, and his companions.

This issue – for a Muslim to carry the Qur'ān to a land of disbelievers – is one about which the scholars disagree: some scholars rule it to be permissible while others rule that it is forbidden. The latter group argues that the Prophet (ﷺ) forbade us from carrying the Qur'ān to lands that are inhabited by the disbelievers because he feared that they might debase, distort, or corrupt it. Ibn 'Umar (رضي الله عنه) related that the Prophet (ﷺ) forbade Muslims from traveling with the Qur'ān to a land of the enemy.[21] In another ḥadīth, 'Abdullāh ibn 'Umar (رضي الله عنه) related that the Prophet (ﷺ) forbade Muslims from traveling with the Qur'ān to enemy lands, fearing that the enemy would get hold of it (i.e. tamper with it or debase it).[22] And in a narration similar to the previous one, the Messenger of Allāh (ﷺ) said, "Do not travel with the Qur'ān, for I do not feel safe about the enemy getting a hold of it."[23]

---

[21] Al-Bukharī (2990) in the *Book of Jihād and Siyar*, Muslim [(1869)-92] in the *Book of Al-Imārah*.

[22] Muslim [(1869)-93] in the *Book of Imārah*.

[23] Muslim [(1869)-94] in the *Book of Imārah*.

The first group of scholars argue that it is permissible to take the Qur'ān to their lands – to spread the message of Islām, to leave the disbelievers no excuses for not believing, and to refer to it for religious rulings that may be needed during travel, but only if the Muslims are strong and can protect the Qur'ān or if there is a pact with the disbelievers that protects the Qur'ān. The two conditions then are that the Qur'ān will remain protected from debasement and that there is hope of deriving benefit from taking it, either to memorize from it, to study it, or to spread its message to others. This view is supported by the end of the aforementioned ḥadīth, in which a reason is given for the prohibition. And this view is stronger, because benefits are achieved while the harm that the Prophet (ﷺ) feared is absent.

And guidance lies with Allāh (ﷻ). O Allāh, send prayers and salutations on Muḥammad, his family, and his companions.[24]

Is it Permissible to Mail a Copy of the Qur'ān to Someone Living in a Land Occupied by Disbelievers?

61-Q: As an employee of the Post Office, I am often faced with foreigners coming to me with packages that contain a copy of the Qur'ān. Most of the time, they want to send it to a country that for the most part is inhabited by disbelievers. Is it permissible to send the Qur'ān to those countries, considering that in Bukhārī and Muslim, Ibn ʿUmar (رضي الله عنه) related that the Messenger of Allāh (ﷺ) forbade Muslims from traveling with the Qur'ān to the land of the enemy?[25]

[24] *Fatāwa al-Lajnah al-Dāi'mah*, *Fatwa* # 3358; ʿAbdul-Razzāq ʿAfifi (Vice-President), ʿAbdul-ʿAzīz ibn ʿAbdullāh ibn Bāz (President).

[25] The *Takhrīj* of this ḥadīth is given in the previous question.

A: All praise belongs to Allāh alone, and may His prayers and salutations be upon Muḥammad, his family, and his companions.

If the package is posted to a Muslim, it is permissible to send it, regardless of whether he lives in an Arab or Non-Arab country and regardless of whether the inhabitants of that country are Muslims or not, because in this situation, it will not come into the hands of the disbelievers: it is not addressed to one of them and there is no danger that we can perceive from them. However, if the country that the Muslim addressee lives in is one that is at war with the Muslims, the copy of the Qur'ān no longer remains safe since the disbelieving authorities might seize it. So in this last case, it is forbidden, and we do not send it, applying the ḥadīth that is mentioned in the question.

And guidance lies with Allāh. O Allāh, send prayers and salutations on Muḥammad, his family, and his companions.[26]

Translations of the Qur'ān, and a Disbeliever Touching the Qur'ān

62-Q: Is it permissible to translate the Qur'ān, for instance, to English, so that disbelievers can read it, for Allāh (ﷻ) says:

إِنَّهُۥ لَقُرۡءَانٞ كَرِيمٞ ﴿٧٧﴾ فِي كِتَٰبٖ مَّكۡنُونٖ ﴿٧٨﴾ لَّا يَمَسُّهُۥٓ إِلَّا
ٱلۡمُطَهَّرُونَ ﴿٧٩﴾

> That (this) is indeed an honourable recital. In a book well-guarded (i.e. *Lawḥ-Al Maḥfūẓ*). Which none can touch but the purified.[27]

A: The Qur'ān is described with the qualities of precision, beauty, perfect style, and flawless cohesion; no translation can be

---

[26] *Fatāwa al-Lajnah al-Dāi'mah*; 'Abdul-Razzāq 'Afifi (Vice-President), 'Abdul-'Azīz ibn 'Abdullāh ibn Bāz (President).

[27] Qur'ān 56:77-79.

equal to the Qur'ān regarding these and other qualities, qualities that are complete and perfect because they describe Allāh's speech. One who attempts a perfect translation is like one who tries to ascend to the heavens without a ladder or a flying machine.

But still, a person who has knowledge may, to the best of his ability, attempt to convey his understanding of the Qur'ān into another language, so that the people of that language may appreciate and learn its meanings, at least the meanings that he understood. There should, however, be no confusion about the matter: his translation is not the Qur'ān, nor is it given the status of the Qur'ān in any way whatsoever. Rather, a translation of the Qur'ān is more similar to a *Tafsīr* book than to anything else, for a *Tafsīr* book is never thought of as being the Qur'ān. That being the case, the following holds true: a disbeliever and one who is in a state of major impurity can touch a translation of the Qur'ān, just as they are permitted to touch a *Tafsīr* book written in Arabic.[28]

---

[28] *Fatāwa al-Lajnah al-Dāi'mah*; 'Abdul-Razzāq 'Afifi (Vice-President), 'Abdul-'Azīz ibn 'Abdullāh ibn Bāz (President).

May Someone Who is in a State of Impurity Recite the Qur'ān?

None May Touch it Except those who are Purified

63-Q: Last night, a few of my friends and I argued whether it is permissible for a person who is in a state of impurity to recite or touch the Qur'ān, or read a book that contains certain verses of the Qur'ān. Please clarify for us the ruling in this issue.

A: All praise is for Allāh, and may His prayers and salutations be upon the last Prophet.

A Muslim who wishes to touch the Qur'ān must purify himself from the smaller and greater impurities (the smaller results, for instance, from passing wind, defecating, or urinating; the greater results, for instance, from engaging in sexual intercourse). The smaller state of impurity requires one to make the Islamic ablution; the greater state of impurity requires one to take a shower. That a Muslim must purify himself when he wishes to touch the Qur'ān is derived from the following verse, which is general in its implications:

لَّا يَمَسُّهُۥٓ إِلَّا ٱلْمُطَهَّرُونَ ﴿٧٩﴾

Which none shall touch but those who are purified.[29]

And the Prophet (ﷺ) wrote the following to 'Amrun ibn Ḥazm:

> "None may touch the Qur'ān except those who are purified."[30]

---

[29] Qur'ān 56:79.

[30] Al-Dāraquṭnī (1/121).

Though he may not touch the Qur'ān, a Muslim who is in the minor state of impurity may read it from memory. It is only the *Junub* (one who is in a major state of impurity) who may neither touch the Qur'ān nor recite it.

And guidance lies with Allāh. O Allāh, send prayers and salutations on Muḥammad, his family, and his companions.[31]

Conferring the Rewards of One's Recitation to the Dead

64-Q: When I am about to read the Qur'ān, should I perform the same ablution that I perform for prayer, or is it permissible for me to recite the Qur'ān without making ablution. Allāh (ﷻ) *says:*

لَّا يَمَسُّهُۥٓ إِلَّا ٱلْمُطَهَّرُونَ ﴿٧٩﴾

Which none shall touch but those who are purified.

So should I purify myself when I want to touch the Qur'ān or is the meaning of the verse restricted to the person who is Junub (i.e. one who is in a major state of impurity, after having performed sexual intercourse or after having had a wet dream)?

And when I am reciting a part of the Qur'ān – even though it may be a small section – may I confer the rewards of that recitation to more than one dead person? Do the dead benefit from this?

A: As for your first question, you may not touch the Qur'ān unless you have purified yourself from both the minor and the major states of impurity, for Allāh (ﷻ) says:

لَّا يَمَسُّهُۥٓ إِلَّا ٱلْمُطَهَّرُونَ ﴿٧٩﴾

---

[31] *Fatāwa al-Lajnah al-Dāi'mah*, *Fatwa* # 2217; 'Abdul-'Azīz ibn 'Abdullāh ibn Bāz (President).

Which none shall touch but those who are purified.

That is, if the *Kitāb-al-Maknūn* is interpreted to mean the *Muṣḥaf*, i.e. a copy of the Qur'ān. This ruling is also based on the ḥadīth of 'Amrun ibn Hazm:

> "None may touch the Qur'ān except those who are purified."[32]

So to directly touch the Qur'ān you must first purify yourself from both the minor and major impurities; however, without purifying yourself, you may carry it if there is a barrier between it and your hand, such as a bag or briefcase.

And as for your second question, there is no proof – as far as I know – which suggests that the Prophet (ﷺ) would read the Qur'ān and then confer the rewards for doing so to the dead, even though some of the people of knowledge have permitted this practice. The correct opinion, then, is that since there is no proof to support this practice, it is not sanctioned. The following are, on the other hand, supported by proof – supplicating for the dead, giving charity on their behalf, performing Ḥajj or 'Umrah on their behalf. So rather than reading the Qur'ān and conferring the rewards for doing so to the dead, a practice that is not founded on the authentic Sunnah, you should do one of the aforementioned deeds, deeds that may be performed on behalf of the dead because they have their source in the authentic Sunnah.[33]

Reciting the Qur'ān Without Making *Wuḍū* (the Islamic Ablution)

65-Q: Without having performed ablution, may one recite the Qur'ān from memory or by actually touching it?

---

[32] Refer to previous question for reference.

[33] *Fatāwā Al-Fawzān*, *Nūrun 'Alad-Darb*. Prepared by Fāyiz Mūsa Abū Shaykhah.

A: To read the Qur'ān from memory, without actually touching it, is a permissible action, for we know from the Sunnah that nothing prevented the Prophet (ﷺ) from reciting the Qur'ān except for *Janābah* (being in a major state of impurity, i.e. after having performed sexual intercourse): He used to recite the Qur'ān after having performed the *Wuḍū*, and he used to recite it without having performed *Wuḍū*.

Nonetheless, an impure person may not touch the Qur'ān, regardless whether he is in a major or a minor state of impurity, for Allāh (ﷻ) says:

لَّا يَمَسُّهُۥٓ إِلَّا ٱلْمُطَهَّرُونَ ٧٩

Which none shall touch but those who are purified.

"Purified" here means those who are purified from physical impurities and those who are purified from disbelief. And the Prophet (ﷺ) wrote to 'Amrun ibn Ḥazm,

"None may touch the Qur'ān except those who are purified."

The *Imāms* agree on this point: that a person in a state of impurity – both minor and major – may only touch the Qur'ān from behind a barrier, such as in a bag or briefcase, or wrapped in a cloth when holding it.[34]

May Children Touch the Qur'ān?

66-Q: Should children be allowed to touch the Qur'ān?

A: The people of knowledge hold opposing views regarding whether one who is in a state of minor impurity (for example, one who has released gas, as opposed to the major impurity, which results from engaging in sexual intercourse) may touch the Qur'ān. One group of scholars rule that it is permissible, arguing

[34] *Fatāwā Al-Fawzān*, *Tadabar-al-Qur'ān*.

that there is no clear proof to the contrary. They also base their view on the fact that all actions or things from this world are permissible in Islām, unless proven otherwise. In other words, the burden of proof lies upon those who say that it is impermissible, and in this issue they have no proof. Another group of scholars rule that it is impermissible to touch the Qur'ān unless one is in a state of purity (i.e. after having performed ablution). Their opinion is founded on a ḥadīth narrated by ʿAmrun ibn Ḥazm (ﷺ), in which the Messenger of Allāh (ﷺ) wrote to him,

> "That only a person in a state of purity may touch the Qur'ān."

And this means someone who has performed the Islamic ablution.

This latter opinion is stronger than the first; although purity (*Ṭahara*) linguistically encompasses both physical and spiritual purity, we have to appreciate that whenever the *Sharīʿah* mentions purity, it is for the most part referring to it in the physical sense. Purity in the spiritual sense means someone who has purified himself from disbelief, meaning the believer as opposed to the disbeliever, and purity in the physical sense refers to one who is not in a state of major impurity and who has performed the Islamic ablution.

What remains, then, is to discuss the issue of children: before attending a Qur'ān class, do they have to make ablution? Or are they exempt because in Islām, the general principle is that children are not held accountable for their actions? Again, the people of knowledge differ: one group of scholars rule that a child doesn't have to make ablution to touch the Qur'ān, because he is not of age, which means that he is not held accountable for his actions. Other scholars rule that he does have to make ablution, and this opinion is certainly not only more careful, but it is also one that carries an additional benefit – children will learn to venerate Allāh's speech. If the teacher has difficulty in forcing the children to make ablution, then he may allow them to touch the Qur'ān using some kind of material as a barrier between it and their hands, a practice that is also permissible for someone who is not in a state of purity.[35]

It is Forbidden for the *Junub* (One Who is in a Major State of Impurity, after Having Performed Sexual Intercourse) to Recite the Qur'ān

67-Q: Is it permissible for one who is Junub to recite the Qur'ān from memory or must he first purify himself by making Tayammum (The substitute form of ablution which is performed in the absence of water, and which is performed by using high ground)?

A: All praise is for Allāh alone, and may his prayers and salutations be upon Muḥammad, his family, and his companions.

The vast majority of scholars agree that it is forbidden for a Muslim to read the Qur'ān when he is *Junub*, even if he reads from memory without actually touching the Qur'ān. In a ḥadīth related by Aḥmad and the compilers of the *Sunan*, ʿAlī (ﷺ) reported that nothing would prevent the Prophet (ﷺ) from the Qur'ān except for *Al-Janābah* (a state of major impurity which results, for instance, from having performed sexual intercourse).[36] And to remove the *Janābah*, one must take a shower; if, for any reason, one is unable to find water or is prevented from reaching it or is sick and cannot use it, one may perform *Tayammum*, a substitute purification that is performed using high ground.

---

[35] Al-Shaykh Ibn ʿUthaymīn.

[36] Aḥmad (1/84,124), Abū Dāwūd (229), Al-Tirmidhī in *Al-Jāmiʿ* (146), Al-Nasā'ī in *Al-Mujtabā* (1/144), Ibn Mājah (596). Al-Tirmidhī said, "This ḥadīth is *Ḥasan Ṣaḥīḥ*." And Al-Ḥāfiẓ ibn Ḥajr said, "Its chain is *Ḥasan*."

And guidance lies with Allāh. O Allāh, send prayers and salutations on Muḥammad, his family, and his companions.[37]

The Audiotape that Contains a Recording of the Qur'ān

68-Q: We know that the Qur'ān is sanctified: none may touch it except those who are purified. What then is your opinion regarding the audiotape that contains a recording of the Qur'ān – may a man who is Junub or a woman who is menstruating touch or carry such an audiotape?

A: All praise is for Allāh alone, and may His prayers and salutations be upon Muḥammad, his family, and his companions.

It is permissible for one who is *Junub* (i.e. in a major state of impurity) or one who is in a similar state to touch or carry an audiotape that contains a recording of the Qur'ān.

And guidance lies with Allāh. O Allāh, send prayers and salutations on Muḥammad, his family, and his companions.[38]

One Who is in a Minor State of Impurity: May he Recite the Qur'ān

69-Q: After having gone to the washroom to defecate, and after having only performed Istijmār (purification not with water, but with clean stones or materials that take the ruling of stones, such as present day toilet paper), is it permissible to recite

[37] *Fatāwa al-Lajnah al-Dāi'mah*, the fourth question from *Fatwa* # 3204; 'Abdul-Razzāq 'Afifi (Vice-President), 'Abdul-'Azīz ibn 'Abdullāh ibn Bāz (President).

[38] *Fatāwa al-Lajnah al-Dāi'mah*, the third question from *Fatwa* # 9620; 'Abdul-Razzāq 'Afifi (Vice-President), 'Abdul-'Azīz ibn 'Abdullāh ibn Bāz (President).

or to touch the Qur'ān? This situation often arises in school, because water may not always be available in school washrooms, and because a student is often required to recite the Qur'ān in class. In such a situation, does one have to make ablution, even though doing so may be difficult?

A: All praise is for Allāh alone, and may his prayers and salutations be upon Muḥammad, his family, and his companions.

It is permissible for someone (whether teacher or student) who has performed *Istijmār* and who has not performed the Islamic ablution to recite the Qur'ān, as long as he is not *Junub* (i.e. in a major state of impurity). However, it is better if he recites after having performed ablution. As for touching the Qur'ān, the vast majority of scholars agree that only one who is purified from the major and minor impurities may touch it. They derive this ruling from the following verse:

لَّا يَمَسُّهُۥٓ إِلَّا ٱلۡمُطَهَّرُونَ ﴿٧٩﴾

Which none shall touch but those who are purified.

They derive the same ruling from another proof as well: the Prophet (ﷺ) wrote to 'Amrun ibn Ḥazm,

"None may touch the Qur'ān except those who are purified."

But if an impure person carries it in a bag or something similar, then it is not considered touching; carrying in this manner is therefore permissible, a ruling that is upheld by *Ḥanbalī* scholars, by Abū *Ḥanīfah*, by Al-Ḥasan Al-Baṣrī, and by a group of other scholars. If a person who is in a state of impurity – whether minor or major – needs to touch the Qur'ān and if there is no water available, he may perform *Tayammum* (Substitute form of purification that is performed using high ground) and then touch the Qur'ān.

And guidance lies with Allāh. O Allāh, send prayers and salutations on Muḥammad, his family, and his companions.[39]

---

[39] *Fatāwa al-Lajnah al-Dāi'mah*, second question from *Fatwa* # 557; 'Abdul-Razzāq 'Afīfī (Vice-President), 'Abdul-'Azīz ibn 'Abdullāh ibn Bāz (President).

In the Absence of Water, May One Recite the Qur'ān Even Though One is Not Purified

70-Q: When I cannot perform purification because neither water nor soil is available, am I sinning if I read the Qur'ān?

A: All praise is for Allāh alone, and may His prayers and salutations be upon Muḥammad, his family, and his companions.

If the situation is as you described it to be, then you may read the Qur'ān without having performed ablution, for Allāh (سُبْحَانَهُ وَتَعَالَىٰ) says:

فَٱتَّقُوا۟ ٱللَّهَ مَا ٱسْتَطَعْتُمْ وَٱسْمَعُوا۟ وَأَطِيعُوا۟

> So Keep your duty to Allāh and fear Him as much as you can.[40]

وَمَا جَعَلَ عَلَيْكُمْ فِى ٱلدِّينِ مِنْ حَرَجٍ

> And He has not laid upon you in religion any hardship.[41]

And guidance lies with Allāh (سُبْحَانَهُ وَتَعَالَىٰ). O Allāh, send prayers and salutations on Muḥammad, his family, and his companions.[42]

Reading the Qur'ān Without Touching it

71-Q: If a Muslim has not performed Wuḍū (the Islamic ablution), may he recite the Qur'ān? What is your proof? Is there disagreement in this issue among the scholars? And if so, which opinion is strongest?

A: All praise is for Allāh alone, and may His prayers and salutations be upon Muḥammad, his family, and his companions.

---

[40] Qur'ān 64:16

[41] Qur'ān 22:78

[42] *Fatāwa al-Lajnah al-Dāi'mah*, second question from *Fatwa* # 1777; ʿAbdul-Razzāq ʿAfīfī (Vice-President), ʿAbdul-ʿAzīz ibn ʿAbdullāh ibn Bāz (President).

If he is in a minor state of impurity (i.e. after having, for instance, defecated or urinated, and not after having performed sexual intercourse, which results in the greater state of impurity), a Muslim may recite the Qur'ān so long as he does not touch it. There is no disagreement among the scholars regarding this ruling since there is no revealed text, neither from the Qur'ān nor the Sunnah, that forbids this practice, and since the original ruling on actions is permissibility, and the burden of proof lies on he who claims prohibition. Nonetheless, it is still better to recite after having performed *Wuḍū* (the Islamic ablution).

And guidance lies with Allāh. O Allāh, send prayers and salutations on Muḥammad, his family, and his companions.[43]

May One Who is Afflicted with Enuresis (Involuntary Urination) Read the Qur'ān?

72-Q: Indeed my heart only finds peace when I read the Qur'ān, and in fact, I do read it often. However, I am afflicted with a condition in which I frequently urinate involuntarily, a condition that affects me at all times. Is it permissible, then, for me to recite the Qur'ān?

A: All praise is for Allāh alone, and may His prayers and salutations be on Muḥammad, his family, and his companions.

Based on your circumstances, you may recite and touch the Qur'ān, even when afflicted with your stated condition. You may even pray when afflicted with your condition, but you must clean yourself and perform *Wuḍū* (Islamic ablution) for every prayer after the time that a given prayer begins. After the time of a prayer has begun, and after you have cleaned yourself and performed

---

[43] *Fatāwa al-Lajnah al-Dāi'mah*, third question from *Fatwa* # 4588; 'Abdul-Razzāq 'Afifi (Vice-President), 'Abdul-'Azīz ibn 'Abdullāh ibn Bāz (President).

Wuḍū, you are not affected by any urine that may come out, which means that you do not have to perform *Wuḍū* again for that prayer. You should wash any body parts or clothes that the urine affects before praying, and your prayer is correct even if some urine comes out while you are praying, for Allāh (ﷻ) says:

لَا يُكَلِّفُ ٱللَّهُ نَفْسًا إِلَّا وُسْعَهَا

Allāh burdens not a person beyond his scope.[44]

وَمَا جَعَلَ عَلَيْكُمْ فِى ٱلدِّينِ مِنْ حَرَجٍ

And has not laid upon you in religion any hardship.[45]

And guidance lies with Allāh (ﷻ). O Allāh, send prayers and salutations on Muḥammad, his family, and his companions.[46]

---

[44] Qur'ān 2:286.

[45] Qur'ān 22:78.

[46] *Fatāwa al-Lajnah al-Dāi'mah*, second question from *Fatwa* # 6984; 'Abdul-Razzāq 'Afifi (Vice-President), 'Abdul-'Azīz ibn 'Abdullāh ibn Bāz (President).

The Menstruating Woman and the Woman Experiencing Postnatal Bleeding: May they Read the Qur'ān?

Women Who are Menstruating May Neither Touch the Qur'ān nor Sit in the Mosque

73-Q: May a woman who is menstruating touch the Qur'ān or recite it? And may she enter the Mosque and sit inside?

A: All praise is for Allāh alone, and may His prayers and blessing be upon Muḥammad, his family, and his companions.

First, based on the opinion of the majority of scholars, a woman may not touch the Qur'ān while she is menstruating. Allāh says:

لَّا يَمَسُّهُۥٓ إِلَّا ٱلْمُطَهَّرُونَ ﴿٧٩﴾

Which none can touch except those who are purified.

And the Messenger of Allāh (ﷺ) wrote to ʿAmrun ibn Ḥazm,

> "None may touch the Qur'ān except for he who is purified."[47]

As for the menstruating woman and the woman who is experiencing postnatal bleeding, they may recite the Qur'ān without touching it; this opinion is correct from the two opposing views held by scholars in this issue, correct because there is nothing from the Sunnah that indicates the contrary.

Second, neither the menstruating woman nor the *Junub* (one who is in a major state of impurity) may stay in the Mosque, not

---

[47] Al-Dāraquṭnī (1/121).

even for a short while. This opinion is held by the majority of Islamic jurists, who base their opinion on the following ḥadīth, which is related by ʿĀ'ishah (ﷺ): The doors of the Prophet's companions were all overlooking or connected to the Mosque, and he (ﷺ) said,

> "Change your doors away from the Mosque (i.e. change the location of your doors, so that when you exit your home, you don't directly enter the Mosque)."

The people didn't immediately respond to the Prophet's orders because each one was hoping that he was an exception to the rule, and that revelation would descend to the Prophet (ﷺ), informing him of that exception. Then the Prophet (ﷺ) said,

> "Change the place of your doors away from the Mosque, for I do not make the Mosque lawful for the menstruating woman and for the *Junub*."[48]

At first glance, the ḥadīth appears to be general in its implications in that it embraces both sitting in the Mosque and simply passing through the Mosque without sitting. However, the ruling of the ḥadīth is not in fact general, because the following verse limits its scope:

يَـٰٓأَيُّهَا ٱلَّذِينَ ءَامَنُوا۟ لَا تَقْرَبُوا۟ ٱلصَّلَوٰةَ
وَأَنتُمْ سُكَـٰرَىٰ حَتَّىٰ تَعْلَمُوا۟ مَا تَقُولُونَ وَلَا جُنُبًا إِلَّا عَابِرِى
سَبِيلٍ حَتَّىٰ تَغْتَسِلُوا۟ۚ

> O you who believe! Approach not when you are in a drunken state until you know (the meaning) of what you utter, nor when you are in the state of *Jannaba*, (i.e. in a state of sexual impurity and have not yet taken a bath) except when traveling on the road (without enough water, or just passing through a mosque), till you wash your whole body.[49]

---

[48] Abū Dāwūd (232).

[49] Qur'ān 4:43.

This is what the verse means: O you who believe, when you are drunk, do not come near places of prayer – i.e. mosques – until you become sobered; and when you are *Junub* (i.e. in a major state of impurity, which results from the two private parts touching or from ejaculation), do not enter a mosque until you have taken a shower, unless by entering, you are only passing through, in which case there is no prohibition. And this same ruling applies to the menstruating woman. And in one narration, Jābir ibn ʿAbdullāh (ﷺ) related that, "When one of us was *Junub*, we would walk through the mosque, but only to pass through."[50] And Zayd ibn Aslam said, "The companions of the Messenger of Allāh (ﷺ) used to walk through the Mosque when they were *Junub*."[51]

And guidance lies with Allāh (ﷻ). O Allāh, send prayers and salutations on Muḥammad, his family, and his companions.[52]

It is Forbidden for the *Junub* and the *Hāyḍ* to Touch the Qur'ān

74-Q: As a teacher of the Qur'ān, may I touch the Qur'ān when my monthly period arrives? Please keep in mind, though, that if I don't teach Qur'ān during that interval, the students will fall behind in my course. And during the course of my monthly period, may I touch books of Tafsīr?

A: It is forbidden for one who is impure (both one in a minor and major state of impurity, and one who is menstruating) to touch the Qur'ān. However, during the course of her monthly period, a

---

[50] Al-Dārimī 1174.

[51] The author of *Muntaqā Al-Akhbār* ascribed this saying to Ibn Mundhir, who related it from Zayd (1/228).

[52] *Fatāwa al-Lajnah al-Dāi'mah*, third question from *Fatwa* # 9620; ʿAbdul-Razzāq ʿAfifi (Vice-President), ʿAbdul-ʿAziz ibn ʿAbdullāh ibn Bāz (President).

female teacher may both listen to her students recite and correct their mistakes. She may even look at the Qur'ān, and though she may not touch it directly, she may turn over the pages using a barrier, such as a tiny stick or something similar. Also, she may touch books of *Tafsīr* and books that contain verses of the Qur'ān. Some scholars have even permitted her to recite the Qur'ān, as she may otherwise forget what she had previously memorized.[53]

While Menstruating, May I Recite the Qur'ān?

75-Q: On the radio program "Nūrun 'Alad-Darb," I heard that it is permissible for a menstruating woman to study and discuss the grammar of the Qur'ān. Now, as a teacher of the Qur'ān's recitation, I have students who come to me from afar, staying with me for short periods of time – may I teach them the rules of recitation by correcting their mistakes or by reciting certain verses while I am menstruating? And what about my students: must they wait until their monthly period ends or is it permissible for them to study during the course of their period? Finally, while I am menstruating, I read books of Tafsīr: is this permissible?

A: All praise is for Allāh alone, and may His prayers and salutations be upon Muḥammad, his family, and his companions.

While you are menstruating, it is permissible for you to recite the Qur'ān, and you may teach the rules of recitation to students who are in the same situation; however, during the course of your monthly periods, neither you nor they may touch the Qur'ān. That being the case, a menstruating woman may still touch books of *Tafsīr* (which is the correct opinion from the two scholarly opinions in this issue) – thus making it easier to refer to certain verses when necessary.

---

[53] *Majmū' Fatāwā wa-Rasā'il*: Al-Shaykh Ibn Jibrīn.

And guidance lies with Allāh (ﷻ). O Allāh, send prayers and salutations on Muḥammad, his family, and his companions.[54]

A Menstruating Woman May Read Books that Contain Verses of the Qur'ān or Sayings of the Messenger of Allāh (ﷺ)

76-Q: Is it permissible for a woman, while she is having her period, to make supplications on the day of ʿArafah, even though those supplications are from verses of the Qur'ān?

A: Both the menstruating woman and the woman who is experiencing postnatal bleeding may recite those supplications that are recommended to the pilgrim and according to the correct view, they may even recite the Qur'ān. No revealed text – the Qur'ān and *Sunnah* – that is authentic clearly forbids these two categories of women from reciting the Qur'ān. It is only the *Junub* (one who becomes impure because of sexual intercourse or because of ejaculation) who is not allowed to recite the Qur'ān, a ruling that is based on ʿAlī ibn Abī Ṭālib's (ﷺ) ḥadīth. As for the menstruating woman and the woman who is experiencing postnatal bleeding, the following ḥadīth has been related concerning them, and it is related by Ibn ʿUmar (ﷺ): "Let not the menstruating woman and the woman experiencing postnatal bleeding read anything from the Qur'ān." However, this ḥadīth is weak because Ismāʿīl ibn ʿIyāsh narrated it from the people of Ḥijāz, and it is known that he was weak when he related from them. So the two aforementioned categories of women may recite as long as they do not touch the

[54] *Fatāwa al-Lajnah al-Dāi'mah*, second question from *Fatwa* # 9402; ʿAbdul-Razzāq ʿAfīfī (Vice-President), ʿAbdul-ʿAzīz ibn ʿAbdullāh ibn Bāz (President).

Qur'ān, whereas the *Junub* may under no condition recite the Qur'ān, at least not until he takes a shower.

The difference between the two is that one is *Junub* for a very short period of time: after having performed sexual intercourse one may take a shower as soon as one wishes, and the matter, so to speak, is in his hands. Even if water is not available, one may perform *Tayammum* (the substitute form of purification that is performed using the earth) and then pray and recite the Qur'ān. On the other hand, the menstruating woman and the woman experiencing postnatal bleeding can do nothing: their affair is in Allāh's hand, i.e. both of them must wait at least a number of days. Because of the long wait, because it is feared that they may forget what they had previously memorized, and because they need the virtues of reciting the Qur'ān and of learning its precepts, they have been permitted to recite the Qur'ān. And even more obvious than that, they may also recite books that contain supplications mixed with verses of the Qur'ān and sayings of the Messenger of Allāh (ﷺ). From the two opinions of the scholars (may Allāh have mercy on them) in this issue, the opinion mentioned here is what is correct.[55]

During the Course of Her Period, a Woman May Read Books of *Tafsīr*

77-Q: When I am not purified, for instance, during the course of my monthly period, I read certain books of Tafsīr (Safwatul-Tafsīr, for example) – am I sinning by doing that? Please inform me of the Islamic ruling regarding this issue, and may Allāh (ﷻ) reward you well.

A: Based on the correct scholarly opinion in this issue, both a menstruating woman and a woman experiencing postnatal

---

[55] *Fatāwā Ibn Bāz, Fatāwā Islāmiyyah* (1/219).

bleeding may not only read books of *Tafsīr*, but they may also recite the Qur'ān itself, as long as they do not touch it. As for the *Junub*, he is categorically forbidden from reading the Qur'ān until he takes a shower, though he may read from books of Ḥadīth or *Tafsīr*. But even with those books, he may not read verses of the Qur'ān that may be written therein, for it has been authentically established that nothing would prevent the Prophet (ﷺ) from reading the Qur'ān except for *Al-Janābah* (i.e. after performing sexual intercourse, and before taking a shower). And in a narration related by Imām Aḥmad, the Prophet (ﷺ) is reported to have said,

> "As for the *Junub*, then no, not even a single verse."[56]

And guidance lies with Allāh.[57]

78-Q: As students in an all-girls Muslim college, we have to memorize 1/30th of the Qur'ān every year. Our exams, however, sometimes coincide with our monthly period; when that happens, may we write the verses we need to memorize on sheets of paper and then revise from them?

A: From the two scholarly opinions regarding this issue, the correct one allows for menstruating women and women experiencing postnatal bleeding to recite the Qur'ān, so long as they do not touch it. They may overcome certain difficulties related to reading by using something, such as a piece of cloth, to act as a barrier between their hands and the Qur'ān. Likewise, they may simply write out the verses they intend to memorize and then rely on the piece of paper that they used, an alternative that saves them from having to use a barrier to change pages of the Qur'ān.

The one who is *Junub*, however, is forbidden from reciting the Qur'ān until he takes a shower, a prohibition that is founded on

---

[56] Aḥmad (1/110), Abū Ya'lā (1/300), Al-Bayhaqī (1/79). In *Mujma Al-Zawā'id* (1/39,40), Al-Haythamī said that the narrators are trustworthy.

[57] *Fatāwā Ibn Bāz, Fatāwā Islāmiyyah* (/219).

an authentic ḥadīth. We cannot use deductive analogy here and say that since both are impure, and since there is an authentic ḥadīth regarding one who is *Junub*, the same ruling applies to the menstruating woman and to the woman experiencing postnatal bleeding. We cannot make this analogy because there is a clear difference between the two: the second category must wait for a long period of time whereas the *Junub* does not – as soon as he has finished performing sexual intercourse, he may take a shower at his leisure. And guidance lies with Allāh (ﷻ).[58]

Menstruation and the Two Units of Prayer One Must Perform when Beginning 'Umrah or Ḥajj

79-Q: How is a menstruating women supposed to pray the two units the pilgrim performs when entering into the inviolable state of Iḥrām? And is a woman permitted to read verses of the Qur'ān to herself, i.e. in a low voice so that no one else hears?

A: The menstruating woman doesn't pray the two units the pilgrim performs when entering the inviolable state of *Iḥrām*. According to the view of the majority of Islamic Jurists, those two units of prayer are Sunnah, while some jurists do not recommend praying them at all. The latter argue that nothing specifically regarding these two units has been related from the Messenger of Allāh (ﷺ). The former group deems it to be recommended based on what has been related from certain *aḥādīth*, such as the Prophet (ﷺ) saying,

> "One came to me from my Lord and said, 'Pray in this blessed valley and say: An 'Umrah in (or with the intention of performing) Ḥajj."[59]

---

[58] *Fatāwā Ibn Bāz, The Book of Da'wā (Al-Fatāwā)* 1/39,40.

[59] Al-Bukhārī in a ḥadīth related by 'Umar ibn Al-Khaṭṭāb (رضي الله عنه) (1534).

The valley referred to is the valley of *'Aqīq* and the Prophet (ﷺ) spoke this statement during his farewell pilgrimage. Some of the Companions related that the Prophet (ﷺ) prayed and then entered into the inviolable state of *Iḥrām*, which is why the majority of scholars recommend that one should enter into the state of *Iḥrām* after having performed prayer, whether that prayer is from the compulsory or the voluntary prayers. One should make ablution and then pray two units. The menstruating woman and the woman who is experiencing postnatal bleeding are not from those who pray, so they should enter the inviolable state of Iḥrām without praying the two units, and it is not legislated for them to make up for the two units once they become purified.

Second, according to the correct view, a menstruating woman may recite the Qur'ān. Scholars agree that she may recite in her heart, without speaking with her mouth; they disagree only regarding whether she may recite out loud. A group of scholars rule that it is forbidden for menstruating women and women experiencing postnatal bleeding to read the Qur'ān or to touch the Qur'ān; they hold that such women must first become purified and then take a shower. Other scholars, as I have mentioned, hold that it is permissible for them to recite the Qur'ān, so long as they do not actually touch it. They argue that the period of waiting is long and that there is no authentic revealed text that forbids them from reciting the Qur'ān, as opposed to the *Junub*, for he may not recite the Qur'ān until he takes a shower, or if he is not able to take one, he performs *Tayummum* (alternate form of purification performed with earth). The proofs given by those who rule it to be permissible are stronger.[60]

80-Q: From what I understand, a menstruating woman is not allowed to touch the Qur'ān, so I was surprised to see some sisters doing just that. When I asked them about it, they said

---

[60] *Fatāwā Ibn Bāz*, the *Book of Da'wah* (*Al-Fatāwā*) 1.135,136.

that it is permissible. What I had previously thought was that a menstruating woman may only touch books of Tafsīr, and not the Qur'ān itself. Please clarify this issue for me.

A: Yes, it is true that no one who is in a major state of impurity – neither the *Junub* nor the menstruating woman nor the woman who is experiencing postnatal bleeding – is allowed to touch the Qur'ān, a ruling that is based on the ḥadīth related by 'Amrun ibn Ḥazm:

> "None may touch the Qur'ān except he who is pure."[61]

The four Imāms agree on this point. A Muslim who is in a major state of impurity may only carry or hold the Qur'ān if there is a barrier separating his hand from it, such as a bag, a briefcase, or a piece of cloth. So he is forbidden from directly touching it. Even though a book of *Tafsīr* contains verses of the Qur'ān, one who is in a major state of impurity may touch it, because a book of *Tafsīr* is not the same as a *Muṣḥaf* (i.e. a copy of the Qur'ān). There is a clear distinction between a *Muṣḥaf* (which contains only the Qur'ān) and a book of *Tafsīr* (which, though it may contain verses of the Qur'ān, also contains words written by man).[62]

Only When Necessary, a Menstruating Woman May Read the Qur'ān[63]

81-Q: Without her actually touching the Qur'ān, is it permitted for a menstruating woman to recite the Qur'ān? And if this is not permissible, is she sinning by teaching her children to read the Qur'ān during the course of her monthly period?

---

[61] Al-Dāraquṭnī (1/121).

[62] *Fatāwā Ibn 'Uthaymīn, Nūrun 'Alad-Darb*. Prepared by Mūsa Abū Shaykhah.

[63] This opinion, which is held by Shaykh Al-Fawzān, is clearly different from the opinions of other eminent scholars, opinions that are given in the previous few questions of this section.

A: A menstruating woman is forbidden from reading the Qur'ān, a prohibition that is inclusive of reading directly from the Qur'ān and reading from memory. This is because she is in a state of major impurity, and anyone who is in a state of major impurity is forbidden from reading the Qur'ān. The Prophet (ﷺ) forbade the *Junub* from reading the Qur'ān, and the menstruating woman, like the *Junub*, is in a state of major impurity, a similarity that leads to a similar ruling.

However, if a woman fears that she may forget those chapters of the Qur'ān that she had previously memorized – especially considering that her monthly period may prolong – then she may read and revise. Her revising the Qur'ān is a necessity and like other situations of necessity, the ruling changes. Similar is the case of the female student whose period arrives during exam time: if she cannot write her exam for Qur'ān class at a later date, she may read or write the Qur'ān for her exam, because were she to leave it, she would harm herself by failing. But even in such a situation, she may only touch the Qur'ān by means of a barrier, something that comes between it and her hands. As for a teacher reading the Qur'ān during her monthly period, doing so is not necessary and is therefore forbidden. And Allāh (ﷻ) knows best.[64]

Books of *Tafsīr*

82-Q: If I am Junub or if my monthly period arrives, may I read religious books, such as Tafsīr books?

A: Those who are *Junub* or who are menstruating may read books of *Tafsīr*, *Fiqh*, Ḥadīth, *Tawḥīd*, and so on. It is only forbidden for them to read the Qur'ān, and that is forbidden only when they are reciting it, and not when they are invoking Allāh

[64] *Fatāwā Al-Fawzān, Nūrun 'Alad-Darb.* Prepared by Fāyiz Mūsa Abū Shaykhah.

(ﷻ) with a supplication that is taken from the Qur'ān or when they are quoting a verse while they are discussing an Islamic issue, for both situations, one in a major state of impurity may utter verses from the Qur'ān.[65]

[65] *Majmū' Fatāwā Wa-Rasā'il* Al-Shaykh Ibn Jibrīn.